SOUTHERN SPAIN
ANDALUCIA
in your pocket

MICHELIN

Travel Publications

MAIN CONTRIBUTOR: ROBIN NEILLANDS

PHOTOGRAPH CREDITS
Photos supplied by The Travel Library:
James Davis Travel Photography 5, 7, 9, 12, 17, 28, 32, 33, 34, 36 (bottom), 37, 38 (top, bottom), 44, 54, 59, 64, 70, 72, 73, 88, 89, 100, 101, 103, 107, 113, 115, 116, 120, 123; The Travel Library 18, 53, 71, 80, 96, 119; A Amstel 93; Stuart Black 77; Tony Boase 24 (bottom); Alan Copson front cover, 61; Philip Enticknap 23, 86, 104; Lee Frost 87; Tony Harris 85; Ian Hunt 41, 110; Paul Moseley 66; Chris Prior 19, 57, 58; R Richardson title page, 30, 81; Erik Schaffer back cover, 10, 42-43, 63, 67, 79, 108, 124; Peter Terry 14, 15, 27, 40, 74-75, 95; David Toase 68; John Welburn 99. Other photos: Greg Evans International/Greg Balfour Evans 91; Charles Fowkes 47; Cayetano Vega Millán 20, 21, 24 (top), 94; Natural Image/Bob Gibbons 36 (top), 50, 82; Natural Image/Mike Lane 49; Museo Julio Romero de Torres Cordoba 76; Williams & Humbert Ltd 45.

Front cover: The Alhambra from San Nicolás; back cover: Costa de la Luz; title page: father and child on horseback

MANUFACTURE FRANÇAISE DES PNEUMATIQUES MICHELIN

Place des Carmes-Déchaux – 63000 Clermont-Ferrand (France)

© Michelin et Cie. Propriétaires-Éditeurs 1996

Dépôt légal Avril 96 – ISBN 2-06-650701-6 – ISSN 1272-1689

MICHELIN TRAVEL PUBLICATIONS
Michelin Tyre plc
The Edward Hyde Building
38 Clarendon Road
WATFORD Herts WD1 1SX - UK
☎ (01923) 415000
www.michelin-travel.com

MICHELIN TRAVEL PUBLICATIONS
Michelin North America
One Parkway South
GREENVILLE, SC 29615
☎ 1-800 423-0485
www.michelin-travel.com

CONTENTS

INTRODUCTION

Welcome to Southern Spain, the region of
Andalucia, *Al-Andalus*, the Land of Light.
When the traveller crosses the Sierra Morena
from Castile or comes down the aircraft steps
at Málaga, he or she is stepping into a very
different kind of Spain, the Spain of the
Moors, a land that is softer, gentler and more
cultured than the barren plateau of Castile
and León to the north. For more than 700
years the Moors ruled Southern Spain.
Although they have been gone for more than
500 years, much of their culture remains in
great cities like Seville, Córdoba and Granada,
in the small villages in the hinterland, and in
the glittering White Towns west and south of
Ronda.

Today, Southern Spain is divided into
eight provinces, each established around a
major city: Almería, Cádiz, Córdoba, Granada,
Huelva, Jaén, Málaga and Seville. Each is
unique and each contributes to the colourful
mix that combines to form Andalucia.

This is a land of sunshine, where strong
colours stand out in the bright light of the
Mediterranean sun, from the golden oranges
in the tree-lined streets of Córdoba, to the
glittering houses of the White Towns, *Pueblos
Blancos*, of Andalucia – places built by the
Moors to withstand the full heat of the midday
sun.

With high snow-tipped sierras and a long
sea-washed coastline, this is a land for all
seasons, perfect for a holiday at any time of
the year. There are championship golf
courses, a wealth of tennis courts, marinas for
the yachting and sailing fraternity and, in the
hills behind the Costa del Sol, there are great
opportunities for walking, riding and skiing.

Southern Spain is a place of music and

dance, where the guitar provides the music for the flamenco, danced here not just for tourists in nightspots, but for sheer joy in cafés and bars. It is typical Spain, yet a place apart. Here there are bullfights and Holy Week processions, *caballeros* on white horses and *señoritas* in *mantillas*. Here you will find sherry *bodegas* and *tapas* bars and throbbing discos, village markets and country fairs. This is the Spain of the tourist posters, but it is also Andalucia and nowhere else in Spain is quite like it.

A view across Montefrio, a typical hilltop village north-west of Granada.

HOW TO USE THIS GUIDE

This guide is divided into four main sections:

Background sets the scene, with an introduction to Southern Spain's geography and landscape, an outline of its rich history and culture, the legends and heroes, and the culture and people of Andalucia today.

Exploring Andalucia starts with a list of the top sights which should be on everyone's holiday check list. The area is divided into the coastal region from the Costa del Sol to the Guadalquivir Delta and then the inland regions of the three great cities of Córdoba, Granada and Seville. Within these regions, the guide provides a tour of the best and most interesting towns and villages, beaches, landmarks, sights and attractions, providing plenty of ideas for excursions and sight-seeing. A gazetteer of places not already mentioned in detail rounds off this section.

Enjoying Your Visit provides friendly, no-nonsense advice on day-to-day holiday activities which can make the difference between a good holiday and a great one – accommodation, eating out, shopping, sports, entertainment and nightlife, as well as information about local festivals and the all-important factor, weather.

A-Z Factfinder is an easy-to-use reference section packed with information, covering everything you may need to know, from tipping to hiring cars, and from using the telephone to drinking water. A word of warning: opening hours and telephone numbers frequently change, so be sure to check with a local tourist office when planning your visit.

A fisherman repairing his nets at Fuengirola on the Costa del Sol.

*Map of south-west
Andalucia (opposite).*

GEOGRAPHY

Southern Spain, the region of Andalucia, is an
area of about the size of Portugal. It is the
second largest region of Spain and scenically
diverse – a range of mountains, a coastline
and a river valley. The main physical features
of the landscape are the high sierras that rise
behind the coast, and the coast itself. The
latter is divided into two parts: the Costa del
Sol, along the Mediterranean, and the Costa
de la Luz, along the Atlantic. The two coasts
meet at the headland of Tarifa. Finally, there is
the great river and delta of the Guadalquivir,
which flows along the foot of the Sierra
Morena, the range of mountains that divides
Andalucia from Castile and Extremadura, and
into the sea at the Coto Doñana.

The valley of the Guadalquivir is a
distinctive feature of Southern Spain, wide
and flat, a great sweep of fertile land
running from north of Jaén to the Atlantic
Ocean, filled with orange groves, vineyards,
olive trees and even cotton.

*Orange groves near
Casares.*

Study a map of Southern Spain more closely and other features start to appear, deep gorges and great reservoirs, or *embalses*, some of them vast lakes, like inland seas, at least until high summer has reduced their water levels. The mountains are high, at an average of around 2 000m (6 000ft), but the Mulhacén peak of the Sierra Nevada soars up to 3 482m (11 424ft), and is snow tipped for most of the year. The other major sierras, the Serranía de Ronda, the sierras of Aracena and Cazorla, and the Alpujarras range between the Sierra Nevada and the sea, are lower but still formidable, though the valleys below the peaks support farms and fruit orchards.

As for the coasts of Southern Spain, they offer a vast expanse of sand in a seemingly endless series of bays, some small, some running for up to 50km (30 miles), each of them backed by resort towns and beach villas, though there are cliffs in the section

There are still many undeveloped stretches of coast in the Costa de la Luz.

between Gibraltar and Cádiz. The estuary of the Guadalquivir supports the Coto Doñana National Park, one of the most important bird and nature reserves in southern Europe.

At times Southern Spain can be a rugged country, where the sun and the sierras can combine to make the countryside a challenge to those who venture into it without a map, a hat and a bottle of water.

HISTORY

Although Southern Spain is, above all, a land of the Moors, Andalucia has a history that can be traced back to remote antiquity. Every race that roved around the fertile Mediterranean shore left some mark. The Iberians, who gave their name to the peninsula, and established themselves in the Guadalquivir valley, near the present site of Seville, are thought to have come from the Sahara and were swiftly followed by the Tartessians, another Iberian

The snow-capped mountains of the Sierra Nevada.

tribe who made their capital somewhere between Sanlúcar de Barrameda and Huelva.

Then came the Phoenicians, who were said to have founded Cádiz in 1100 BC and Málaga in 1200 BC and certainly established trading posts along the southern shore. The roving Greeks inherited these ports when they took over the sea trade of the Mediterranean. Hamilcar Barca, the Carthaginian general and father of Hannibal, conquered the Iberians but the Carthaginians were in turn driven out by the Romans, who

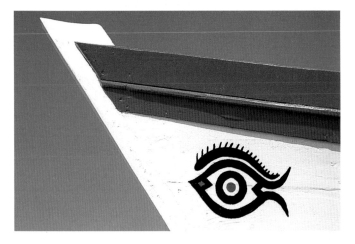

arrived in 206 BC and made Iberia a Roman province, Hispania.

Southern Spain has a great seafaring history.

All this is history, or prehistory, but there is mythology as well: Hercules came this way, on one of his Labours, seeking the Golden Apples of the Hesperides, which were probably the oranges of Andalucia. The Torre de Jerez in Seville has an inscription saying 'Hercules built me, Caesar surrounded me with walls and towers; the King Saint took me'. The Roman name for the region was Baetica.

A number of famous Romans came from Andalucia, like the philosopher Seneca, who was born in Córdoba in 4 BC, and two emperors, Hadrian and Trajan. When the Roman Empire collapsed in the 5C AD the Visigoths arrived and made it the capital of their conquests south of the Pyrenees. The Visigoths ruled in Spain until the Moors arrived in 711 AD.

Moors and Al-Andalus

Once again Andalucia played a part in the history of Spain. The first Moor to arrive in the peninsula was a minor chieftain called el Tariq. He established himself on a distinctive single mountain – or *jebel* – just north of the straits which therefore became known as the Jebel el Tariq – or Gibraltar.

These were the Umayyad Moors, from Damascus, who had been spreading the Muslim religion along the north African shore for 100 years before they arrived in Spain. Once there they spread north rapidly and by 732 AD they had overrun most of the peninsula. Then began the long fight back, the Christian War of Reconquest, which went on for over 700 years until 1492, when the last Moorish kingdom in Spain, the Kingdom of Granada, was conquered by the Catholic monarchs of Castile and Aragon, Ferdinand and Isabella.

The time of the Moors was a Golden Age in Spain, not just in the south; a look at the Moorish monuments which remain make that much very clear. The Moors built the *Mezquita* in Córdoba, the Alhambra and Generalife gardens in Granada, the Alcazar and Giralda in Seville and the white towns

which adorn the countryside. They irrigated the land and introduced crops such as orange and cotton. Under the Moors, Andalucia flourished and prospered.

The Moors were poets, doctors and philosophers, while the Spaniards to the north of the Sierra Morena were simple armoured warriors. When Abd el Rahman was the Emir of Córdoba at the end of the 8C, the city had a thousand or so mosques. His dynasty, the Umayyads, ruled *Al-Andalus*, as it then was, until the end of the 10C when a warrior vizier, Al Mansur, overthrew the

A tiled historic scene depicting Cádiz at the Plaza de España in Seville.

ruling Emir. Under Al Mansur, the Caliphate of *Al-Andalus* reached new heights of power, but after his death in 1002, the Caliphate disintegrated and finally collapsed (1032) and a number of smaller kingdoms sprang up in *Al-Andalus*. During this period the Almoravids and then the Almohads arrived from Africa to join in the Muslim struggle against the Christian north. These new arrivals were true warriors and they soon took over the land of the Umayyads and ruled *Al-Andalus* in their place.

Al-Andalus has a way of softening people, and the Almoravids soon succumbed to the good life and soft living of the peninsular, coming to terms with the Christians. Trade between the two halves of Spain flourished

The Court of Lions in the Alhambra, Granada.

and civilization leapt forward; the Moors gave shelter to the persecuted Jews and encouraged advances in medicine and science. One Jewish resident of Córdoba, the philosopher Maimonides, even became personal physician to the mighty Saladin at the end of his life in Egypt.

The Almohads were made of sterner stuff and when they arrived in the 1150s the wars between Christian and Moor began again. The Almohads wisely elected to avoid the soft temptations, and, having taken over *Al-Andalus* in their turn, they ruled it from their African capital of Marrakech.

A Trading Nation

In the long run, though it took centuries, the small Moorish kingdoms of *Al-Andalus* were doomed. The pressure from the north was relentless, and one by one the kingdoms fell to the Christian kings. The Crusader King, or King Saint, Fernando III, entered Córdoba in 1236 and stripped the mosque of the *Mezquita* of its gold and silver but left the structure intact. This conquest did not satisfy his ambition and Seville fell to Fernando III 12 years later, in 1248.

Then the pace of the Reconquest slowed. It was not until 1485 that Ronda surrendered, Málaga lasted another two years. The last of the Moorish kingdoms, the Kingdom of Granada, survived until 1492, when Boabdil surrendered to the Catholic kings. After that the Spanish queen, Isabella, had time to listen to a Genoese seaman, Christopher Columbus, who had been frequenting the Court and telling wild tales about a sea route to the Indies.

After the Reconquest, Andalucia continued to flourish for a while, nourished

The Cathedral in Seville. This is the largest Gothic church in the world.

by the trade with the Indies. Treasure ships from Mexico and Peru were obliged to dock at Seville, and great Spanish lords such as the Duke of Medina Sidonia, commander of the Spanish Armada in 1588, acquired estates in the old Moorish kingdoms. A

feature of this time were the raids by English
sailors such as Sir Francis Drake, who
attacked Cádiz in 1587, to 'singe the King of
Spain's beard'.

*Fishing is still an
important industry
in Andalucia.*

　　Around the great cities new forms of
agriculture were developed, producing wine
and grain and olives, while the cities became
trading centres for the Mediterranean, but
the people in the countryside slowly sank
into poverty over the next two centuries.

18

During the Peninsular War – or, as the Spanish call it, the War of Independence – (1808-1814), Andalucia saw a mixture of triumph and disaster. The junta of Andalucia inflicted a great defeat on the French general Dupont at Bailen in 1808, and held off the French besieging Cádiz.

This century, the Spanish Civil War of 1936-1939 did further damage, but since then, despite the dominance of the Franco regime, Andalucia has developed a new role as one of Europe's great holiday playgrounds. If some of the development has not been for the good, that is now changing. It has always been the genius of Andalucia to absorb new influences and transform them into something better.

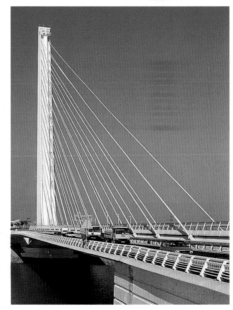

Puente del Alamillo, Seville.

19

Architecture of Andalucia

With its mixture of Moorish and Christian culture, Southern Spain possesses a wealth of varied architectural styles and some very splendid buildings from the early medieval period through to the late Renaissance and the baroque. The two main forms of Andalucian architecture with Moorish connections are the Mudejar and the Mozarabic. **Mudejar**

Arches in the Mezquita at Córdoba, showing the fine carving.

buildings, or the Mudejar style, refers to work carried out by Moorish craftsmen working under Christian direction. The Christians took Seville in the 13C so this style can be found in early medieval buildings in Seville and elsewhere in the Guadalquivir valley, and was still popular in the 16C.

Mudejar work can usually be identified by the use of brick and heavily decorated wooden ceilings. **Mozarabic** art or architecture, on the other hand, is work done by

Christians living under Moorish rule and is rather more ornate and heavily decorated. The post-Conquest period is noted for great Gothic cathedrals, like those in Seville and Granada, which often stand on the site of former mosques and often incorporate parts of the mosque into the structure. Spain was wealthy after the discovery of the New World and the buildings erected in the 16 and early 17C are often in the rich Renaissance style known as **Plateresque** ('*plata*' means silver).

The **Mezquita** at Córdoba, which next to the Alhambra, is the finest Moorish building in Spain, dates back to the Caliphal period. This magnificent building went up in stages between about 740 AD and 1 000 AD. The Mezquita embraces all the influences which are Andalucia: re-used Roman pillars; double Visigothic arches; Mudejar decoration and a Plateresque choir.

Southern Spain is also rich in **military architecture**. There are great city walls at Almería, Granada, Carmona and Castellar de la Frontera, and a

A view through an archway in the Mezquita at Córdoba.

great quantity of castles, Moorish, Christian, or a mixture of the two. The Alcázar in Córdoba, the walls of the Alhambra, and the castles at Carmona and Tabernas are some of the best.

PEOPLE AND CULTURE

Thanks to the cinema, and works like Bizet's *Carmen*, the culture and folklore of Andalucia is often confused with the culture of other parts of Spain. This can lead to the assumption that all Spaniards play the guitar, sing flamenco and dance *sevillanas* to the click of castanets.

The culture of Spain is far too diverse for that single image to have any validity and every region makes its own unique contribution to Spanish folklore and culture. Although such a folklorique event as flamenco dancing – or, more correctly, flamenco singing, since it is actually the song and music rather than the dance – is taken to be typically Spanish, flamenco music is the music of Andalucia. It is drawn from gypsy *gitano* sources, mixed with some Moorish vivacity, touched with some Spanish sadness and combined into a haunting song which is typically Andalucian, especially when spiced with some heel-stamping, skirt twirling, the rattle of the castanets and the occasional '*olé!*'.

Flamenco is usually performed by professional troupes, but in any bar, disco or fiesta where the Andalucians gather there will come a moment when modern music stops and people rise to dance *sevillanas*. The *sevillana* is a graceful, twirling dance, without the vigour of the flamenco but very much a part of Andalucian, and especially Sevillana life, danced by local people of every age, not to entertain the tourists but for sheer pleasure.

Seville and Málaga are great places to see Andalucian dancing, and the *tablaos* or performances of Andalucian song and dance. At these events the dancers and singers wear Andalucian costume: the men in black, with high-heeled boots and flat sombreros, the

The April Fair in Seville.

women in tight-bodiced dresses with flounced skirts and a multitude of petticoats.

Fairs and Processions

These splendid costumes appear again at the various Andalucian *ferias*, or country fairs, where the horsemen (*caballeros*) and their ladies often arrive on horseback, with the lady sitting up behind the saddle of her escort, a marvellously romantic way to get about. Fairs, often combined with horse or agricultural shows, take place all over Andalucia. The best are held in Jerez de la Frontera in May, in Seville around Easter time, and especially at the pilgrimage of El Rocío, to the shrine of the Virgin of the Dew, at Whitsuntide. The local tourist board will be able to advise visitors of any *feria* or *romería* (pilgrimage) taking place during their visit.

The Catholic religion has a strong hold on

An effigy of the
Sacred Heart.

the people of Andalucia, best seen during
Holy Week – *Semana Santa* – or Easter Week
processions in Seville. Seville is the capital of
Andalucia and crowds from all over the
province flock here during Holy Week to take
part in a powerful and even disturbing
experience. During Easter Week, the
confraternities or brotherhoods in each
quarter of the city take it in turns to organize
a procession through the streets of the town,
with statues, tableaux of the saints and
martyrs, and bands. Great crowds of penitents
carry the often very heavy tableaux, escorted
by further torch-bearing penitents and
members of the confraternities, masked in
tall-cowled hoods that remind some visitors of
the Spanish Inquisition.

Horse Fairs and Bullfights

For most of those taking part, and for many of the locals looking on, Holy Week processions are a deeply religious and emotional experience. Those of a less serious outlook might find the fair which often follows the *Semana Santa* processions rather more enjoyable and equally colourful. Andalucians love horses and a great number of people and horses assemble in Seville each April for the annual fair. The accompanying bullfights are among the most famous in Spain, and most of the spectators in the great Maestranza bullring of Seville Plaza de Toros will be in Andalucian costume.

The excitement and dangers of a bullfight.

Bullfighting, like flamenco, is not confined to Andalucia, but this is the home of the great *toreros*, the *matadors* or bullfighters; this is where the rules of the modern bullfight were first established, in Seville and Ronda by the Romero family, and the finest and fiercest fighting bulls in Spain are bred on the farms of Andalucia and Castilla. Andalucia has also produced some of the great bullfighters, like the renowned Manolete, who was killed in the ring in 1947, aged 30, and Manuel Benítez, who comes from Córdoba and so is known as *El Cordobés*. Every town has its *torero*, whether he is a star from the past, a current reality, or a hope for the future. In Seville, Morante de la Puebla is on his way to replacing living legend Curro Romero in the hearts of its citizens.

Bullfighting is not to everyone's taste. Those who want to get to grips with the culture and folklore of Andalucia can hardly afford to miss a bullfight, but those who have objections to what is, by any standards, a bloody and dangerous activity should probably give it a miss.

MUST SEE

To pick just ten sights to see in Southern
Spain is far from easy, but the following
should not be missed, partly because they
are well worth visiting, and partly because
getting to see them will take you through
some of the most striking parts of Andalucia.

The Alhambra★★★, Granada

The Alhambra, or 'al-Hamra' – the Red
Fortress – of Granada is one of the essential
sights of Spain, a peerless triumph of Moorish
architecture, a pleasure dome that continues
to attract visitors five hundred years after the
last King of Granada, Boabdil, was driven
from his home here. Apart from the voices of
the visitors the main sound in the Alhambra
is the tinkle of water, but the main attractions
are the courtyards, such as the **Court of
Lions**, the **Myrtle Court**, or the **Hall of the
Ambassadors**. It could take days to explore all
of the Alhambra, but do not miss these.

The Cathedral★★★, Seville

All the cathedrals of Andalucia are worth
visiting and all contain something unique.
The cathedral in Granada contains the
tombs of Ferdinand and Isabella, the
Catholic monarchs who took the city from
the Moors, but the cathedral in Seville
contains the splendid **tomb of Christopher
Columbus**, and the famous **Giralda
Tower★★★**. The cathedral in Seville is also
the largest Gothic church in the world.

Ronda★★

The attractions of Southern Spain are by no
means all man-made. In Ronda, for
example, the great gulf of the Tajo gorge
cuts the town in two. The **old bridge** over the

Intricately carved arches in The Alhambra, Granada.

gorge contains a prison and spans a vertiginous gulf, cut through the rock of the **Serranía de Ronda** by the Guadalevín river. Across the gorge from the bullring lies the **Ciudad**, the old part of Ronda, full of shady squares and medieval houses. Ronda is a fine town, but the **bullring★** here, which contains a fascinating **Bullfighting Museum**, is a perfect gem. It is possible to walk out into the centre of the ring and get some idea of what it might be like to be faced with an enraged Miura bull, but the real reason for

entering the bullring at Ronda is that the
building is stunning. The ring was built in
1784 and is said to be the oldest in Spain; it
is certainly the most beautiful.

Cliff-top houses in Ronda overlooking the Tajo gorge.

Generalife Gardens★★, Granada

The Moors loved gardens, fountains and flowers, and every old Moorish house still has its cool courtyard. The finest Moorish gardens in Andalucia are those of the Generalife which is only a short walk from the Alhambra through an avenue of cypresses.

The Mezquita★★★, Córdoba

The Mezquita of Córdoba was, and remains, one of the wonders of the Islamic world. Entering the Mosque is like entering a huge forest, so thickly are the interior columns gathered, like the trunks of trees. Surrounded by a courtyard full of orange trees, the Mesquita was left intact after the Christians took the city in 1236, but in 1523, the archbishop of Córdoba decided to build a cathedral in the centre of the great mosque, an act which outraged his sovereign, the Emperor Charles V. 'What you have built,' he told the archbishop, 'could have been built anywhere. What you have destroyed was unique in this world.'

The Mezquita is still the central attraction of the city of Córdoba, together with the **Judería**★★ (Jewish Quarter), which, with its white alleyways and flower-filled courtyards, is now a World Heritage Site.

Santa Cruz district★★★, Seville

This district is a maze of small streets wending their way between tiny squares, amidst whitewashed homes decorated with sumptuous forged iron gates revealing shady, flower filled courtyards. Hours could be spent wandering around this area, chancing upon new discoveries and temptations, hopelessly yielding to its endless charm.

Albaicín★★, Granada

Below the Alhambra and separated from it by the Darro valley, the Albaicín is the Moorish quarter of town with its maze of narrow white streets, shady squares and numerous churches. From the San Nicolás terrace, there is a breathtaking **view★★★** of the Alhambra and the Sierra Nevada.

Baeza★★ and Úbeda★★

These were the first two Andalucian towns to be reconquered by the Christians after the battle of Navas de Tolosa. It is difficult to

separate these two provincial towns, a few kilometres apart, dotted with Castilian style historic buildings and churches, and whose architectural style and university vocation have earned them the nickname of 'the little sisters of Salamanca'. Being a land of transition between the austerity and dignity

Arcos de la Frontera perches on the edge of a cliff face.

of Castille and the carefree radiance of
Andalucia, they are well worth a detour
through the Jaén olive groves.

The Royal Chapel★★ (Capilla Real), Granada

The Royal Chapel was built by order of the
Catholic kings who wanted to be buried in
this town, which was a symbol of the
reunification of Spain by the Christians.
Built in flamboyant Gothic style, along with
the **marble tombs★★★** of the royal couple it
houses a **museum★★** with an extraordinary
collection of paintings by Flemish (Van der
Weyden, Memling), Italian (Botticelli) and
Spanish (Berruguete) masters.

The White Towns★

The White Towns, or *Pueblos Blancos,* of
Southern Spain were built by the Moors to
fight off the intrusive rays of the sun. Narrow
streets offer plenty of shade, white walls
reflect back the rays of the sun, and every
leafy courtyard has its fountain. The White
Towns are therefore practical in this hot
climate, but they are also very beautiful,
especially when seen from a distance,
glittering across the valley.

Every householder in a *Pueblo Blanco* is
obliged by law to whitewash his house at least
once a year, but most of them do more than
that, filling the windowsills and courtyards of
their homes with flowers and plants. The bulk
of the White Towns lie around **Ronda★★**, with
Olvera, Ubrique, **Setenil★**, **Grazalema★**, Gaucín,
Benadalid and **Acos de la Frontera★★** among
the most attractive. Rather more touristic but
still very attractive is the White Town of
Mijas★, perched above the Mediterranean,
between Marbella and Málaga.

THE COAST AND ITS HINTERLAND

Southern Spain has two coasts, the Costa del Sol and the Costa de la Luz, and each has its own special attractions. The Costa del Sol, on the Mediterranean shore, has more tourist developments, with plenty of resorts, villa developments and an expanding number of marinas and golf courses. The Costa de la Luz, however, on the Atlantic side of Tarifa, is more open, given over more to vineyards and arable farming. This makes it somewhat quieter, but the beaches on the Atlantic coast are better than those on the Costa del Sol.

Costa del Sol★

The Costa del Sol runs from Almería to Gibraltar and is one long tourist development, especially along the section from **Málaga★** to Estepona.

Best Beaches Recommending a 'best beach'

A typically busy beach at Estepona, on the Costa del Sol.

Smoked fish on sale at the beach in Fuengirola.

on the Costa del Sol is difficult. Many are crowded and overlooked by apartment blocks or hotels, and the sand can be grey and gritty. That said, the sea is warm and the sun certain, and if what you want is a tan or somewhere for the children to paddle, these beaches will certainly do, though the hotel or apartment swimming pool will probably be cleaner. The best beaches are those at the resorts of **Torremolinos**, or **Fuengirola**, though the beaches between the two will be quieter and cleaner. Those who insist on perfect beaches for their holiday should probably head for the Costa de la Luz.

Those who like windsurfing should head for **Tarifa**, west of Gibraltar. The strong and reliable winds off the headland attract top windsurfers from all over Europe.

Best Resorts – Fuengirola, Estepona, the jet-set resort of **Marbella★★**, Torremolinos (once Britain's favourite 'place-in-the-sun') have all been surpassed by newer, more fashionable places. **Málaga★** is more than a port and airport; the old town centre is certainly worth exploring. The best resorts along the Costa del Sol today, with the possible exception of **San Pedro de Alcántara**, which is more a residential town than a holiday resort, tend to be the smaller ones like Puerto Banús and **Puerto Duquesa**. These small, modern, but well-designed places were erected after the ghastly effects of high-rise concrete had become all too obvious.

Puerto Banús★ was built in the early 1970s, and rapidly became *the* place for the younger smart set, especially for those who had tired of the attractions of Marbella. The resort offers sailing, windsurfing and jetskiing during the daytime, as well as smart

The marina at Marbella.

restaurants, noisy bars and even noisier discos at night. **Puerto de la Duquesa** is smaller and quieter, a place for families, with a large marina, handy beach, golf course and plenty of small restaurants.

Today, the big attraction of the Costa del Sol, west of Málaga, is the golf courses: splendid year-round places like **Sotogrande**, often the site of major international tournaments, but always willing to welcome visitors.

East of Málaga the nicest place of all is **Nerja★**, which has a fine castle, some remarkable **caves★★** and a palm-shaded corniche known as the *balcón de Europa*. The coast road is attractive and overlooked by medieval watchtowers erected to warn against the Barbary corsairs. Finally, away at the western end of the Costa del Sol lies the British colony of **Gibraltar**. 'The Rock', as it is known, has some interesting sites, such as the old naval cemetery where the dead of the battle of Trafalgar lie buried.

Inland from the Costa del Sol

If the coastline of the Costa del Sol is not to your taste, there are many compensating attractions just a few minutes drive away inland. The Moorish town of **Mijas★**, west of Málaga, is the first among these, perched on a terrace 500m (1 640ft) above Fuengirola and the sea. Mijas is a tourist trap, but an agreeable one. It is well kept and sparkles in the mountain air. The streets are full of bars and restaurants, with donkeys on hand to carry you up the steep, narrow parts. Those who have a morning to spare should spend it in Mijas, while those with a full day to spare should press on through the village of **Coín** to famous Ronda.

A cable car makes its descent in Gibraltar.

Ronda★★

Situated in the heart of the *Serranía* and divided in two by the great gulf of the **Tajo gorge** – a 150m deep abyss cut through the rock by the Guadalevín – Ronda is an impressive **beauty spot★★**. Two different areas can be distinguished: the **Ciudad** (City) or oldest part of Ronda, and the **Mercadillo**, linked by the **Puente Nuevo★**, a bridge which was built over the ravine in the 18C.

A walk through the **Ciudad★★** is full of pleasures. This former Arab town, whose original roads remain virtually intact, will transport you back to the time of *Al Andalus*. Don't miss the **Colegiata**, notable for its gallery, a former mosque whose minaret

The stalactites and stalagmites of the Nerja caves are lit up to provide a breathtaking spectacle.

A street café in Mijas.

The church of Santa María la Mayor in Ronda still has parts of the mosque it replaced.

Right: Map showing Ronda and some of the White Towns inland from the Costa del Sol.

Puente Nuevo Bridge in Ronda.

remains, and the Arab baths at the foot of the town. Along the way, you will pass the **Salvatierra** palace with its Renaissance façade before returning to the centre via the Roman Bridge.

The Mercadillo is famous for its **bullring★** (*see* p.27). The gardens of the Hotel Reina Victoria – on the edge of the gorge – where Rilke used to stay, will seduce romantics with their melancholy charm.

Harsh and sensual, Ronda developed from the blending and clashing of civilisations that created Andalucia out of Al-Andalus...

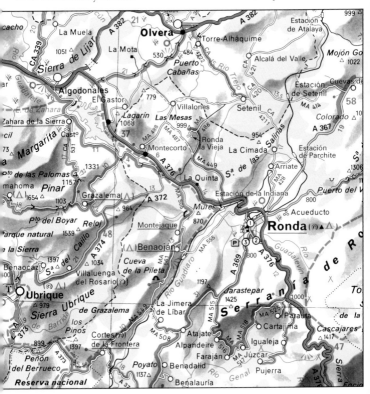

The Serranía de Ronda

The Ronda mountains are home to a rich wildlife and to one particularly unusual plant: the **pinsapo**, a conifer which dates back to the Quaternary. Here you will undoubtedly come across cork oaks, and the route of the **White Towns★**. But don't miss a visit to the **Cueva de la Pileta★**, where cave paintings 25 000 years old can be found

Arcos de la Frontera★★, perched on a rocky spur, is worthy of a visit because of its

The village of Benadalid in the hills south-west of Ronda.

exceptional **location★★**. Leave your car at the bottom of the village as the roads are very narrow. You won't regret the climb up to the centre of the town, the **Plaza del Cabildo**, from where a magnificent **view★** can be enjoyed. And a refreshment stop at the Parador in the square will compensate for the effort.

Jaén Province

Coming from Castille, the **province of Jaén** is the gateway to Andalucia. The only access is through the **Despeñaperros** pass.

It opens out onto a landscape dotted with olive groves, the criss-cross of their silvery embroidery stretching over the red earth as far as the eye can see. The province has two Meccas of Spanish identity: **Las Navas de Tolosa**, where the victory gained in 1212 over the Almohades by the allied armies of Castille, Aragon and Navarra opened the door to the reconquest of Andalucia, and **Bailén** where, in July 1808, Napoleon's army was vanquished in the War of Independence.

Although **Jaén** offers little of interest, there is an enjoyable detour to **La Carolina**, a colony of originally Swiss settlers founded by Charles III in the 18C, which was rapidly decimated by malaria. The angular way in which this tiny city was planned, resembles that of a medieval fortified town. After

The cathedral at Baeza.

The lovely village of Cómpeta, near Nerja (following pages).

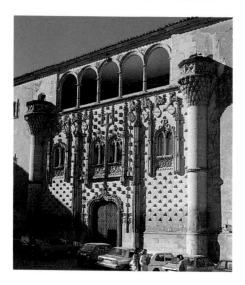

The ornate 15C façade of the Jabalquinto Palace at Baeza in the Jaén Province.

passing through the mining town of **Linares** (famous as the place where the bullfighter Manolete met his death in 1947), do not fail to visit **Úbeda★★**, whose **old quarter★★** is worth a visit, as is the **plaza Vázquez de Molina★★** where the Parador is situated and, not far away, the church of **El Salvador★★**, whose sumptuous edifice was designed by Diego de Siloé. A few kilometres further on is **Baeza★★**, the first Andalucian town to be retaken from the Muslims in 1227, which became a university town in 1595. The best way to enjoy the charm of its **historic centre★★★** is to wander past the golden-brown fronted residences, through squares such as the **Plaza del Pópulo★** and the Plaza de Santa María as well as the splendid **Jabalquinto★** palace, a wonderful example of late Gothic architecture (*see* p.30).

Jérez de la Frontera★

At the mouth of the Guadalquivir, the ancient vineyards producing the famous Jérez or Sherry, are located. The town of **Jérez de la Frontera★**, (it is one of the homes of flamenco, where the famous *cantaor* Antonio Chacón was born) is worth a detour, especially for its famous **bodegas★** or sherry cellars where the renowned *fino* is matured which, when aged, becomes *amontillado*; and the sweetest *palo cortado* and *oloroso*, a dessert wine.

A demonstration of sherry pouring will almost certainly be included in a tour of one of the many bodegas of Jerez.

The names of the producers are witness to the fact that the vineyards are in the hands of families of British (Willliams, González Byass) or French origin, such as Domecq, who arrived in the south-west at the beginning of the 19C. A visit (best organised

through the tourist office) is, of course, accompanied by a sherry tasting and if you are driving, you should beware continuing your journey immediately, as these wines are between 17º and 24º proof.

Jérez is also the Andalucian horse capital, the so-called *cartujano* horse. **The Andalucian School of Equestrian Arts★**, established in 1973, gives an amazing show entitled '**How Andalucian horses dance**'★★ every Thursday morning and gives demonstrations of horsemanship and dressage.

In passing, admire the baroque façades of the town's historic buildings (**Casa Domecq★**, de los Ponce de León, de los Pérez Luna) and of the Colegiata. A curious **clock museum★★** may also be of interest.

Further south is the small town of **Puerto de Santa María★** which is primarily the port from where Jérez wines are exported, especially to Britain which absorbs 40% of production. This tiny, industrious and lively town also has its sherry cellars, such as those of the Osbornes, famous for placing the silhouette of a bull on all Spanish hill tops in order to advertise their product. The 'Osborne bull' is today considered a national monument.

This journey through sherry country would not be complete without a visit to the port of **Sanlúcar de Barrameda★** at the mouth of the Guadalquivir, from where Magellan set off on his voyage around the world. It is the home of *manzanilla* which is made like sherry but it has a slightly salty taste due, they say, to the sea breeze. Be careful though: manzanilla also means camomile – and you may be surprised to be served a herbal infusion as an aperitif when outside this region!

An inseparable complement to tapeo, *the subtle and full-bodied* vinos de solera *loosen tongues while giving you the real flavour of Andalucia.*

Cádiz is said to be the oldest city in Europe.

Cádiz★

Cádiz is located on a tip of a narrow peninsular. Founded in 1100 BC by the Phoenicians, it is the oldest city in Europe. Its prosperity dates from the 18C when it acquired the monopoly of trade with the Americas after the silting up of the Guadalquivir obliged Seville to renounce this claim. Its name is linked to many historic events: the disaster of Trafalgar in 1805 and its resistance to Napoleon's troops, who never managed to occupy it despite an interminable siege. Representatives of regional government set up their **Cortés** here under the dome of the church of San Felipe Neri and adopted a constitution in 1812. In 1823, the taking of the Trocadero fort left its mark on Parisian place names. Today, Cádiz is a modern and lively town, with a port and naval docks. A walk along the **Paseos Marítimos★**, with their **gardens★** overlooking the ocean, is a must. The **Cádiz Museum★** is worth a visit for its archaeology section and for the **Zurbarán paintings** dating from the artist's best period.

GUADALQUIVIR DELTA

Leaving Seville by the motorway towards Huelva, take the exit for Bolullos del Condado. The local white wines, which are dry and light, are perfect with fish and seafood. Head for Almonte, and then on to **El Rocío**: an unusual white village built on the very edges of the marshes, with roads of ochre sand reminiscent of cowboy westerns, particularly as it is not uncommon to catch sight of a horse tied up in front of a house.

El Rocío comes to life every year at Whitsun when a *romería* is held in honour of the **Virgin of the Blanca Paloma**. It is probably the biggest pilgrimage in Spain since an estimated one million pilgrims make the journey. Often in traditional Andalucian dress, on horseback or in lavishly decorated carts drawn by oxen, participants come from all over Andalucia, following the routes of annual migration and sometimes setting off ten days before. Needless to say, the wine which flows on the makeshift campsites, the sound of the drums which incessantly beat and the flamenco songs sung around camp fires, make this pilgrimage a kind of itinerant *feria* which reaches a frenzied pitch on the night which brings the Virgin from her sanctuary for a long procession.

Doñana

El Rocío has an observation post from where you can discover the bird and animal life of the **Doñana National Park★★**. The Information Centre of **El Acebuche,** based in an Andalucian *cortijo*, has an interesting exhibition on the history and ecosystem of the park. From there, four-wheel-drive vehicles (booked in advance) will enable the park's three areas to be discovered in a half-day tour. To the west are the **cotos** or hard sands covered with bushes and a few trees, including pines; next the **marisma**, an area of swampy ponds, a paradise for birds, and, on the coast, the moving sand dunes which advance roughly six metres each year.

This, the largest national park in Spain, covers some 73 000 hectares. Under the influence of both the Mediterranean and the Atlantic and near to the African coast, it is on the migratory route of numerous species of birds and one of their stopping places, hence its classification as a protected reserve in 1969.

These landscapes, not unlike those of the Camargue, are the permanent home to more than 125 species of bird, along with 150 others which spend several days here

Flocks of the elegant greater flamingo can be seen at the Doñana National Park.

during their annual migration: egrets, pink
flamingos, harriers, imperial eagles and
many varieties of duck. You may also be able
to see mammals: deer and wild boar are not
uncommon and lynx can also be found.
Bring binoculars and a tele-photo lens.

West from Doñana

Following the road you arrive at
Matalascañas, the first resort on the Costa de
la Luz. Situated between the park and the
sea, this is an excellent starting point
(including on horseback) for expeditions by
nature lovers. A straight road along the coast
(hidden by enormous dunes) through the
pine forests (where there are a number of
campsites) will take you to **Mazagón** where

Marshes in the
Doñana National
park. In the
background lies
El Rocío.

the steps of Columbus can be retraced by visiting the **Palos de la Frontera** and neighbouring **Moguer**, situated in a strange lunar landscape. It was from the port of Palos, now silted up, that he set off on his first voyage on 3 August 1492 and it was to Moguer that he returned in March 1493 after the discovery which was to change Andalucia's destiny.

Not far away stands the monastery of **La Rábida**. Whilst staying here Columbus managed to convince an astronomer monk, Antonio de Marchena, of the possibility of reaching the Indies via the west. Eight years later, Marchena in turn persuaded Isabella the Catholic to sponsor the navigator's venture, something which few people believed in. Only a cloister now remains of the monastery which Columbus knew.

Capital of the province, and situated at the mouth of the Río Tinto, **Huelva** – the starting point for many expeditions to the New World – is a busy industrial port due to the mineral wealth of the hinterland. A huge statue of **Christopher Columbus**, who is particularly honoured here, stands in the port.

As far as the border with Portugal, the Costa de la Luz offers long sandy beaches scattered with resorts such as **Punta Umbría**, **Ayamonte★** or **Isla Cristina**. The beaches are beautiful but the rough ocean limits them to surfers and windsurfers rather than those looking for a family beach holiday.

Inland

Further to the north, in the foothills of the Sierra Morena, **Aracena★** is worth a detour. This typical mountain village (at an altitude of 1000m/3 280ft) is overshadowed by the ruins of a castle of the Knights Templar, whose church has a minaret decorated in a similar style to that of the Giralda. But Aracena is above all known for its **Gruta de las Maravillas★★★** whose concretions have been brightly coloured with metal oxides. If you like spectacular sights, you will not be disappointed. The **Sierra de Aracena★★** is verdant and many inhabitants of Seville come here to escape the summer's heat, especially along the banks of the reservoirs which have been formed by dams. Here you will cross through the impressive opencast mines of **Riotinto★★**: copper mines which were abandoned in 1986 and gold and silver mines which are still being exploited. Take advantage of this mountain visit to try the famous **Jabugo** ham *jámon serrano*, the best in Spain, before looking at the castle and the mosque of **Almonaster la Real★**.

The Legado Andalusí

This foundation, born out of the keenly contested World Alpine Skiing Championships in the Sierra Nevada in 1995, has the aim of revitalising the Andalucian economy based on a culture and tourism project aimed at making the architectural, scientific, craft and gastronomic heritage of *Al-Andalus* better known. Amongst its actions are the building of *Al-Andalus* roadways which, from Lisbon, Madrid, Marrakech or Damascus converge on Granada; the production of quality publications; and the organisation of thematic exhibitions and videos.

Contact address: Calle Molinos 65, 18009 Granada, ☎ 958 22 59 95, fax 958 22 86 44. They have a shop in the Corral del Carbón, in Granada.

A farmer driving sheep along a dusty road. This more traditional way of life is still a familiar sight inland from the coastal resorts.

THE THREE GREAT CITIES OF ANDALUCIA

Córdoba★★★

A Roman city, capital of emirs and caliphs, situated on the banks of the Guadalquivir in the centre of a fertile region devoted to livestock farming, olive groves and cereal crops, Córdoba has remained a symbol of tolerance and harmony between the three monotheistic cultures: Jewish, Christian and Arab. Capital of the *Al-Andalus* emirs from 719 onwards, and seat of the independent

dynasty of the Omayyads from 756, the city was the cultural and spiritual beacon of the West until its Reconquest in 1236, even after it lost its political importance with the fall of the caliphate in 1070 when it was rejoined to the kingdom of Seville. Córdoba was then a town of around 500 000 inhabitants with dozens of schools, universities and libraries. With the Reconquest and the massive exodus of the population began the slow decline of the city.

The interior of the Mezquita with its many columns (about 850) made of white stone and red brick.

Today it is difficult to imagine its previous importance and perhaps the best way to gain an idea would be to visit the archaeological site of the **Azahara Medina (Madinat al-Sahra)**★, 8km (5 miles) along the road to Palma del Rio. This was a city built by the first caliph, Abdelrahman III. Begun in 936 and destroyed by the Berbers of Al-Mansur less than a century later, this new town was to become the political nerve centre of the caliphate. The mosque and town, gardens and the remains of an imposing Alcazar are spread over three terraces dominating the plain, the construction of which required 10 000 workers. The site was rediscovered in 1911 and some of the rooms are slowly being restored: some are austere, (house of the Vizirs (Dar al-Wuzara)), some grandiose, (Abdelrahman's lounge), decorated with plant motifs.

Córdoba is best visited on foot: the historical centre is sufficiently small and it is practically impossible to take a car in. A visit can be gruelling in the summer, when Córdoba is oppressively hot. Why not go at the beginning of May during the **courtyard festival**? This is when the courtyards are open to the public and the owners do their best to fill them with blooms.

A tour of the centre of Córdoba should begin with the **Calahorra** tower, a bastion constructed in the 14C to defend the approach to the Roman bridge. From there you will gain a superb view of the old city, dominated by the enormous mosque with the cathedral piercing right through its centre. On crossing the bridge and the Puerta del Puente (an 'Arc de Triomphe' built during the reign of Philippe II), you will discover the incontestable jewel of the

town, the imposing **Mezquita-Cathedral★★★**
(*see* p.29). The mosque was begun in 780
andsuccessively enlarged by the addition of
new naves until 987 when it took on its
current dimensions. You enter by the
Orange Tree Court, the former courtyard of
ablutions which is surrounded by porticoed
galleries and planted with orange trees.
Inside the mosque you will discover a
surprising forest of columns (more than
850) supporting two tiers of red and white
striped arches adorned with capitals, some
taken from the former Visigoth cathedral
which stood on this spot. Do not miss the
sumptuous and skilful decoration of the
mihrab★★★. Opinions are divided regarding
the cathedral; it is late Gothic in style and
was erected in the middle of the mosque,
thus altering the perspective and tranquillity
of this colonnade (some of the columns
were destroyed and ogival vaults covered
some of the rooms). But the building would
undoubtedly have been considered
remarkable wherever it had been built and
the juxtaposition of these two completely
different forms of architecture provides
some of the charm of the mosque today,
although it is a shame not to be able to see
the monument as it was originally conceived.

From here you progress naturally to the
Judería★★, or Jewish quarter, with its white
alleyways filled with hundreds of flowerpots
hanging from the walls (the Callejón de las
Flores is the best example) and its
marvellous courtyards. It is a good place to
find something to eat (try the famous
salmorejo of Córdoba, accompanied by a *fino*
from Montilla-Moriles) and there are plenty
of souvenir and handicraft shops (leather
and filigree silver). There is also a medieval

*Endless columns
and the
sumptuously
decorated mihrab
bear witness to the
splendour of the
Córdoba caliphate.*

synagogue, one of three remaining in Spain. Nearby, the **Zoco** is a large square around which handicraft stalls are set up and where concerts are held in summer. One side is occupied by the **Taurin Municipal Museum**, housed in a 16C mansion. Mementoes of the Córdoban masters are exhibited here.

You rejoin the Guadalquivir at the Christian **Alcázar★**, built in the 14C. For three centuries this building was the headquarters of the Spanish Inquisition. Here the archaeological remains of Roman Córdoba can be seen but the highlight has to be its Arab style **gardens★**. Strolling further on you will discover Christian Córdoba as symbolized by the poignant **Cristo de los Faroles**, emblem of the city: admire the **fernandine churches★**, built after

View along the Puente Romano at Córdoba towards the Mezquita.

57

Ferdinand III had reconquered the town. There were 14 of them, all built in a primitive and austere Gothic style, to which today **San Miguel★**, **San Lorenzo★** and Santa Marina de Aguas Santas bear testimony. Not far from the latter, the sumptuous **Palacio de Viana★★** is well-known for the beauty of its 12 courtyards and the garden around which it is built. From the **Plaza de la Corredera,** rectangular and surrounded by porticos housing shops and bars full of hustle and bustle, you will rejoin the **Plazuela del Potro** where a hostel described by Cervantes in *Don Quixote* remains. On this square you will find the Fine Arts Museum (a collection of Spanish paintings) and the **Julio Romero de Torres Museum★**, devoted to the works of this Córdoban artist. The **Archaeological Museum★★**, which is in the Palace of the Páez, is worth a visit just for its Roman artifacts, but also its extremely beautiful collection of Muslim decorative art, part of which comes from Medina-Azahara, is a must, particularly the marvellous bronze **stag★** (el cervatillo).

The Arabic style gardens at the Alcázar, Córdoba (below left).

Granada★★★

The whole world dreams of Granada. But rarely does reality improve on the dream. Such is the case with Granada and the lines of the poet Jorge Icaza, on seeing a blind man, must be quoted for their accuracy: *Give him alms, my wife/ For there is nothing worse in life/ Than the misfortune of being/ Blind in Granada.* It is, of course, the magnificence of the Nasrid Palace of the Alhambra, this miracle of balance, grace, light and beauty to which Granada owes its reputation.

A rooftop view of Córdoba.

Granada has an exceptional setting, built on forested hills in the centre of a fertile *vega* with the backdrop of the snow covered peaks of the Sierra Nevada. This, along with the wealth of its history and monuments, and its intellectual tradition, all combine to make it one of the essential World Heritage Sites, as designated by UNESCO.

The splendour of Granada was born out of the decline of Córdoba. After the Reconquest of 1236, a large part of the Córdoban population sought refuge in Granada where Mohamed Ibn Ahmar founded the nasrid dynasty, under the authority of King Ferdinand III. From 1238 to 1492, the town came to know unprecedented prosperity in both economic and artistic spheres. Internal dissent was later to facilitate the task of the Catholic kings, when Boabdil surrendered the keys to the city on 2 January 1492, after a six month siege. But the true decline only began after the expulsion of the Moriscos in 1609.

The **Alhambra★★★** (Red Fortress), is the heart of the city, a rich mixture of palaces, fortifications, and pleasure domes, with fine buildings, gardens, ponds and fountains all set together in glorious profusion. Before entering Nasrid Palace, the centrepiece of the Alhambra, take time to visit the **Generalife★★**, the summer residence of the emirs.

This will give a beautiful view of the Palace. The charm of this somewhat decayed architecture (here represented by a number of quite simple pavilions) is unbelievable and the gardens are marvellous. The intricate water system, channelling water from the Sierra Nevada to the water jets whose power was designed in such a way that 'their noise did not conceal the birds'

songs'. This detail gives an indication of the extreme sophistication of this last Moorish dynasty (*see* p.29). Returning to the Alhambra visit the Presentation Room where, with supporting examples, you will learn about the different types of decoration and the techniques used in the **Nasrid Palace★★★**, built in the 14C. In particular you will learn that the columns have no more than a decorative function, thus their elegance and finesse. Soak up the

View across the Albaicín district of Granada.

atmosphere as you tour the Palace. Let yourself be carried away by the subtle interplay of space and light, with its rooms spread out around *patios* and the repeated views over the Albaicín quarter and the Sacromonte hill. Rooms such as the **Ambassadors**, undoubtedly the most sumptuous but also the **Two Sisters** and the **Abencerrajes** (where these were massacred), marvellously decorated with floral motifs and calligraphy which makes the stones seem like a veritable book. There is the splendid **Court of Myrtles** and, especially, the **Court of Lions** with its marvellous overhanging wings. Along the way, the curious Italian paintings depicting hunting and fighting scenes on the ceiling of the **Kings' Room** bear witness to the changes which took place between Christian and Muslim worlds. Be sure not to miss the sumptuous royal baths. Leave the Palace by the **Partal Gardens★★** where a few towers and the remains of a mosque are to be found, along with the **Palace of Emperor Charles V★★**, built by one of Michelangelo's pupils, Pedro Machuca: undoubtedly a key Renaissance work for its simplicity (a circle inside a square) and its very Florentine allure. It houses a **Spanish-Muslim Museum★** whose principal treasure is the **jarrón azul**, a work in blue ceramic, 1.32m high, which adorned the Sala de las Dos Hermanas of the Alhambra, and the Fine Arts Museum which exhibits paintings and sculptures often of religious inspiration. The **Alcazaba★** is the oldest part of the Alhambra (13C), a work of military design and giving splendid **views★★** over the town. On certain nights during the summer, some of the rooms and courtyards of the Alhambra are illuminated

Enjoy the Generalife, with its refined Andalucian gardens...and breathtaking view of the Alhambra.

and may be visited.

Lying below the north side of the Alhambra and spreading over a hill beyond the Darro river, is the **Albaicín★★**. This was the Moorish part of the town (it has retained its topography) but after 1492 was taken over by the aristocracy. Taking the Carrera del Darro from the Plaza Nueva, you pass in front of the **Arab baths★** (El Bañuelo), and from here you can visit the Archaeological Museum in the Casa Castril (which has a notable plateresque **great door★**). Unless you wish to climb the hills by donkey (there is a 'donkey rank' at the end of the walk),

The Court of Myrtles in the Alhambra, Granada.

take the Cuesta del Chapiz to enter the district (it is quite steep).

You will find beautiful white houses concealing superb gardens (the **cármenes**), monasteries and churches, popular squares and, from the San Nicolás terrace, a superb **view★** of the Alhambra in its verdant setting at the base of the Sierra Nevada, which is often snow covered. Try the specialities of Granada in one of the restaurants: broad beans with ham or Sacromonte omelette. Further up are the 'clubs' of the Sacromonte Gypsies, few of whom remain, where flamenco is first and foremost a commercial business.

A view of the Alhambra from the Generalife Gardens.

Return to the modern town by the Calderería, where honey cakes, mint tea, dress and language of the locals, often Moroccan, will transport you temporarily back to the time of Boabdil.

After this the busy and noisy lower town, crossed by its two main axes, the Gran Vía de Colón and the calle Reyes Católicos, may at first seem somewhat disappointing. But the district around the cathedral is worth a stroll, even if only for the marvellous **Capilla Real**★★ or Royal Chapel (*see* p.31). The **cathedral**★ is remarkable above all for its size. The Zacatín, a business area, will lead you to the **Alcaicería**. This is a former silk market which was rebuilt in the 19C, today a veritable souk of souvenirs and handicrafts. Nearby, the **Corral del Carbón**, a former caravanserai (inn) beautifully restored to a very simple design, houses the Tourist Office and craft shops. The lively Puerta Real preserves the memory of the 'tertulia' (regular gatherings discussing such topics as poetry, flamenco, bullfighting, even politics; normally held in a café, a Spanish institution!)

Next to the *Chikito* restaurant is *El Rinconcillo* where Falla and Lorca used to meet. Nearby the Bibarrambla and Mariana Pineda squares are an ideal stop for a drink before continuing your walk. Granada has numerous churches: enthusiasts of baroque architecture should visit the church of **San Juan de Díos**★, heavily gilded, before visiting the **Cartuja**★ (Carthusian monastery) whose **vestry**★★ is absolutely extraordinary, or the monastery of **San Jerónimo**. Granada is an important university town: the courtyards of the Conservatoire of Music or of the Faculty of Law, bordered by a botanical garden, make you wish you were a student again!

The Campo del Príncipe – a vast square at the foot of the Alhambra has a whole side full of restaurants, or try one of the taverns along the calle Navas or down the alleyways around the Plaza Nueva.

The Alpujarras mountains are scattered with picturesque small villages.

Around Granada – 30 kms away, the **Sierra Nevada★★** (*see* p. 87) is a beautiful place to go walking in the summer. The hills of **Las Alpujarras★**, with their picturesque villages, and Lanjarón (*see* p. 84), are also worth a visit. The house where Lorca was born, in **Fuente Vaqueros**, is now a museum.

Seville★★★
Capital of Andalucia, Seville requires a visit of several days: apart from splendid monuments it is here that the Andalucian way of life is taken to an extreme. The sumptuous processions of Holy Week and the dynamism of its festivals are famous and something to be experienced. Avoid the

heat of summer as far as possible and explore the centre, which is not all that large, on foot.

Seville became Christian once more in 1248 and added gold from the Americas to the splendours of the Arab era. Thus the city has a wide range of architectural styles which bear witness to these opulent times.

It is the **cathedral★★★** and the **Giralda Tower★★★** which first attract visitors. From the top – 70m (230ft) up – there are marvellous **views★★★** of the town , bristling with steeples and minarets, and you will also be able to see the layout of the imposing cathedral itself, designed as a challenge to Christendom (*see* p.26). The peaceful Court of Oranges is a remnant of the former mosque, of which the Giralda was the minaret. The cathedral is the largest Gothic church in the world. Its appearance is quite heavy but the interior, whose height is surprising (flamboyant vaults reach 56m/184ft), reveals a number of treasures such as the immense hispano-flemish **altarpiece★★★** depicting scenes from the life of Christ in the Capilla Mayor. The plateresque **Capilla Real★★**, reserved for worship, is not easily accessible to tourists. But in the many chapels and the treasure house you can see paintings by Murillo, Valdés Leal and Zurbarán.

Sherry of the finest quality is found in Jerez.

Nearby, a building constructed by Juan de Herrera houses the Indies Archive. Original manuscripts written by Columbus, Magellan and Hernán Cortés are on exhibition here. The next essential sight of Seville is the **Alcázar★★★** (signposted as the **Reales Alcazares**), a masterpiece of Mudéjar art. (Entry tickets are from an automatic machine – make sure you have change.)

This grandiose palace was built by Pedro the Cruel in 1362 on the site of an Almohad alcázar – of which there are a few remains – using Arab workers from Granada. Enjoy the delicateness of the decorations in the Patio de las Doncellas and the splendid Salon de Embajadores before taking a walk in the magnificent **garden**★. The exit leads to the **Santa Cruz district**★★★, the former medieval Jewish quarter. You could spend a long time strolling around this labyrinth of white streets which open into tiny squares of immense charm, discovering here or there a half open door onto a courtyard of flowers,

The patio in the Pilate's House, Seville.

Stroll though Santa Cruz and its maze of white alleyways, enjoying patios decked with flowers and jam-packed tascas along the way.

especially as several bars provide an opportunity to quench the thirst (*see* p.29).

The **Hospital de los Vénérables★** is a fine example of Seville's baroque architecture; headquarters of a cultural foundation, it houses exhibitions. Do not let a fear of getting lost prevent you from continuing along the roads or amongst the stalls of craftsmen at work (bookbinders, saddlers, cobblers), where you will discover churches with coloured façades and **Pilate's House★★** (Casa de Pilatos), a pseudo-reconstruction of Pontius Pilate's house in Jerusalem. Pastiche it may be, but what a surprising mix of Mudéjar, Renaissance and flamboyant Gothic styles. The courtyard's **ceramic tiles★★** alone make the detour worthwhile.

Why not take one of the horse-drawn carriages waiting around the cathedral to continue your tour? (ask to see the official price list). They will take you to the greenery of the **María Luisa Park★★**, well worth seeing in summer. Along the way, the baroque doorway of the San Telmo Palace, seat of the Andalucian government, can be seen, as can the University, established on the premises of the Tobacco factory so dear to readers of *Carmen*. Further on, curious pavilions built for the Ibero-American exhibition of 1929 (some house museums) and the famous **Plaza de España★**, semi-circular with its 58 benches of ceramic tiles, each one depicting a Spanish province. From here follow the Guadalquivir to the **Tower of Gold**, bastion of defence dating from the Almohades era; the bullring of the Real Maestranza built in 1760 and bearing the colours of the town's buildings: white underlined with yellow; the **Hospital de la Caridad★** (Charity), founded by Miguel de Mañara in an attempt to make

amends for a dissolute life. The church houses some particularly macabre pictures of Valdes Leal.

Beyond the river, the popular district of **Triana** provides an opportunity for buying some superb ceramic tiles. Some come from the **Cartuja**, a Carthusian monastery converted into a ceramics factory in the 19C and a focal point of the Expo 92 exhibition. This exhibition initiated the development of this new district, where public administration is due to move to. As for the **Parque de los Descubrimientos** (Park of Discoveries), it retains the pavilions of Expo 92 and has been transformed into a theme park (Isla Magica), enjoyed by both adults and children.

A walk in the El Arenal district is a must, where there are a multitude of taverns to discover and you can surrender to the art of eating tapas which, in Seville, has reached unrivalled levels. Or, if you prefer, go back to the Plaza Nueva where the Town Hall stands, with its marvellously sculpted eastern face.

Seville's Tower of Gold, with a sightseeing boat on the Guadalquivir.

Children in traditional colourful dress.

The Santa Cruz district and the entrance to the Jewish Quarter, the Judería.

Look at the buildings, a surprising mixture of styles and yet, by some strange alchemy, pure Seville. Now you are entering Seville's shopping area, its squares and streets, in summer covered by a canopy in order to protect passers by from the heat of the sun. The **Calle Sierpes**, with its trendy or deliciously outmoded boutiques is the nerve centre of the town. It leads to the commercial centre where the town's department stores are found.

The **Fine Arts Museum★★★**, housed in a monastery, brings together a magnificent collection of Spanish painting, with excellent works by Murillo and striking Zurbaráns.

But the best thing to do is to let chance take you where it will. Go past the Basilica of the Macarena (with one of the most valued Virgins in the city) and cross through a popular district dotted with churches whose steeples are often former brick minarets, to reach the convent of **Santa Paula★**, founded in the 15C.

Or, strolling further on, enter the vast **plaza del Salvador** and be surprised to find it teeming with people. Tiny bars are the cause

The Giralda Tower in Seville (left).

of this gathering of people who drink standing up in the square, animatedly discussing everything and nothing. It is the beginning of an evening devoted to *tapeo*, an activity which must be undertaken with all due seriousness. The best way is to follow the crowd – why are some bars empty whilst you can hardly get into the one next door? Such are the mysteries of word of mouth and of the *movida*, a phenomenon which moves the

crowd from one district to another. As an accompaniment to a *fino*, ask for the tapas which are written on the slate: these are the house specialities; in this way a full, varied and economical meal can be eaten on the move, without even noticing it.

For a rest and a change from sight-seeing, try the boat tour from Seville to Sanlúcar de Barrameda – have lunch there and return in the afternoon.

The Plaza de España in Seville was built in the 1920s as part of the Ibero-American Exhibition.

Flamenco and Sevillana

Spain is the country of the dance. It can boast many other art forms but the dance is one that permeates every level of Spanish society, and is found in all regions, from the *jota* of the Aragón region and *sardane* from Catalonia, to the flamenco and *sevillana* of Andalucia. The *sevillana* is a local dance, created in Seville. Such local dances can be found in other cities, another Andalucian example being the *malagueña*, which comes from Málaga. The *sevillana* and the *malagueña* are popular dances, learned and danced by people all

The sevillana is still a vibrant part of modern Andalucia.

over Spain because they are graceful, exciting and fun. Flamenco is quite different. Flamenco is all drama, fire and passion.

True, pure flamenco is an art form, and the people who dance it well are as dedicated as any ballet dancer. To learn flamenco and give yourself to its rhythms can take years, and requires long training, much practice and total commitment.

The three elements in flamenco are the music, the song and the dance. The musician must be able to follow the dance, and the song must express the soul of flamenco, as much as the dance does with its stamping, whirling and rattle of castanets. If everything works well, the dancer will enter an almost trance-like state, *duende*, a state of possession by the dance and the music. This state can spread to the audience who will break into bouts of hand-clapping in time to the music, and greet the end of the dance with rapturous '*Olé*'s'!

As to the origins of flamenco, opinions vary. It is certainly a very old dance,

A flamenco dancer in full flight.

and some trace it back to 1C AD, when the Jews were expelled from Jerusalem, taking a form of this dance with them into exile. Others claim it is a gypsy dance. The Greeks and the Moors have also been credited with inventing it, but, whatever its origins, the flamenco today is a product of Southern Spain, and a flamenco performance is an essential feature of any visit to Andalucia.

OTHER PLACES GAZETTEER

Algeciras

An old town and port, Algeciras is now rather spoiled by the nearby oil refineries. Founded by the Moors in 711 AD, it overlooks the bay of Algeciras and the Rock of Gibraltar, becoming a major trading centre and a garrison town. The Roman aqueduct and 8C chapel 'Our Lady of Europe' are worth a visit. Ferries leave here daily for Tangier and Ceuta.

Alhama de Granada

This large village is set on the edge of a deep gorge on a plateau east of **Málaga** and is chiefly famous as the sight of the penultimate battle between the Christians and Moors in 1482.

Almería

Arab *Al-meriya* (mirror of the sea) is today the capital of a lively province whose main activities are agricultural (fruit and vegetables grown under glass). The white town is dominated by its **Alcazaba★** (8C-10C), notable for its **gardens★**. The **fortified cathedral★** is worth a visit. The province of Almería, often barren, does hold some interest: the **Cabo de Gatas★★** (marine reserve and paradise for divers); the pretty

Arab village of **Níjar**; not far from Tabernas, in a desolate, red and barren landscape reminiscent of a Technicolor Colorado, is **mini-Hollywood**, with sets used in the shooting of many 'spaghetti westerns'.

Almodóvar del Río★★

Almodóvar lies in the Guadalquivir valley, beyond the ruins of Medina Azahara. It is a quiet, picturesque Moorish town, except on the second Sunday in May when the town celebrates the pilgrimage of the Virgin of Fatima.

Almonaster la Real★

Some 30km (18 miles) west of **Aracena**, Almonaster la Real is well worth a diversion. The church was built by Moorish craftsmen and contains all kinds of local additions using stone from Roman ruins.

Álora★

Alora has an unusual castle, filled with the town cemetery. The town itself cascades down the slope from the fortifications on the ridge.

Andújar★

This town lies east of Córdoba in an area noted for its sunflower and olive oil crops. Many houses date from the 15C and 16C. The church of Santa

Looking through the Giant's Arch over Antequera. This was built as a triumphal arch for Philip II in the 16C.

The white-walled village of Casares.

María has a painting, *Christ in the Garden of Olives*, by El Greco. About 30km (19 miles) north of Andújar is a 13C sanctury, **Santuario de la Virgen de la Cabeza**. It is now an important place of pilgrimage each April.

Antequera★

This is one of the finest of the smaller towns north of **Málaga**, close to a soaring rock, known as the **Lovers' Rock** (Peña de los Enamorados). It is now a market town, but visitors are mostly attracted by the prehistoric **dolmen**★ burial chambers in the **Cuevas de Viera, Menga** and **Romeral**, the parador, and the narrow streets in the well-preserved Moorish Quarter. The nearby rock formations, known as the Torcal de Antequera, are full of interesting wildlife.

Baena (SE of Córdoba)

Baena's olive oil is the best in the world, or so say the Córdobans. The town is also well-known for its Holy Week: the drums beat for 48 hours on end!

Benadalid

Below the sierra, south and west of Ronda, Benadalid is a large village. The cemetery is set in the centre of the ruined castle, and is completely surrounded by crenellated walls.

Cazorla, in the Jaén province, has an impressive setting.

Carmona★★ (E of Seville)

A Roman city perched on a rock overlooking the Guadalquivir plain, Carmona is a town in which to pass an unforgettable evening. The Parador, based in the palace of Pedro the Cruel, is currently closed for renovation but there are plenty of romantic hotels:

The idylically placed town of Grazalema.

La Casa de Carmona has a strange charm! Wander its white streets as night falls, perhaps with piano music drifting through open windows, or silent squares. The town is surrounded by Roman walls and has several churches and monasteries (some famous for their cake shops) worthy of interest. A vast Roman necropolis has been discovered on the outskirts of the village.

Casares★

One of the most picturesque villages in the province of Málaga, in the **Sierra de Bermeja**, 12km (7½ miles) from Estepona, and is a jewel of a place with white houses, flower-decked streets and tiny plazas, with the mountains as a perfect backdrop.

Castellar de la Frontera★
(N of Algeciras)

The historic centre of this town, enclosed within the walls of its fortress, is a fine example of town planning from the nasrid era.

Écija★ (W of Córdoba)

The 'frying pan of Andalucia', it goes without saying that a visit during August is best avoided. The village is, however, worth a visit for its towers, former church steeples (including the **Torre de San Juan★**), its Baroque residences decorated with courtyards and the **church of Santiago★** whose Gothic altarpiece is worth the detour.

Cazorla★

The province of Jaén gets fewer tourists than the coastal regions but this little village in the **Sierra de Cazorla★★★** is worth seeking out, with its two castles set in spectacular **scenery★**.

Galaroza

This minute village in the **Sierra de Aracena★** is another good walking centre.

Gaucín

Between Ronda and Gibraltar, Gaucín is one of the finest of the White Towns, and was once a favourite weekend retreat for officers of the Gibraltar garrison. There is a good walking trail to **Castellar de la Frontera** and **Jimena de la Frontera**.

Grazalema★

West of Ronda, on the road to El Bosque, and set under the rocky bulk of the Serranía, this is the place to buy woollen cloaks or *zerapes*, ponchos, or the brightly coloured blankets (*jarapa*) for which the weavers of Grazalema are famous in Southern Spain.

Guadix★

Famous for its **cave dwellings**, which are still inhabited by modern troglodytes. This town, under the Sierra Nevada, boasts a pretty **cathedral★** (**baroque façade★**), the church of Santiago with its richly decorated façade and a Plaza Mayor dating from the time of Philip II. Nearby, the troglodyte village of **Purullena** is well-known for its pottery.

Itálica★

Not far from Seville, on **Santiponce** territory, are the ruins of a Roman town with several mosaics and the remains of an amphitheatre, one of the largest in the Roman world.

Jabugo

Jabugo, in Huelva province, close to **Almonaster la Real**, is famous for producing the finest mountain ham, *jamón serrano*.

Jaén

In the middle of a vast sea of olive groves (**view★★** from Calvo Sotelo's Alameda), the town has an **Archaeological Museum★** and **Arab Baths★★**, the most important remaining in Spain. The **cathedral★★** has superb stalls sculpted by students of Berruguete, hidden behind the lovely Baroque façade.

Jimena de la Frontera

(SW of Ronda)
Dominated by a castle established by the Romans and rebuilt in the 13C. It is right in the heart of the Alcornocales Nature Park (cork oak), the last remnant of the pre-Iberian forest.

La Calahorra (SE of Guadix)

At first it appears an austere, massive **fortress** perched on a promontory and flanked by mighty towers – nothing to indicate the subtlety and refinement of the richly decorated Renaissance court-yard that lies inside the ramparts!

Lanjarón

A spa town, in the **Alpujarras★** hills, close to Granada, noted for its restaurants and pure water, producing much of Spain's mineral water. A good base for exploring the Alpujarras hills.

Paseo del Parque, Malaga

Málaga★

The town where Picasso was born (a museum devoted to him has been created in the palace of the Counts of Molina) remains an extraordinary site, even if too many skyscrapers have disfigured the skyline. The best view of the bay is had by climbing Gibralfaro Hill, crowned with the Arab-built walls of the **Alcazaba★** (which houses a parador). The adventurous should explore **El Perchel**, the old flamenco district.

Matalascañas

This is the nearest resort to the wildlife reserve of the **Doñana National Park★** (*see* p.48), set on a long white sandy beach between the Guadalquivir and the city of Huelva. Matalascañas is new, noisy and international.

Mojácar★

In the east, near Almería, Mojácar encircles the top of a hill a short distance from the coast. A classic moorish village with many white-washed houses, providing excellent views of the surrounding countryside, and now a popular holiday base.

Osuna★★(E of Seville)
Town of the famous dukes, amongst the most powerful in Spain, it has a pretty **historical centre★** with Baroque residences and a palace. The Collegiate houses paintings by **Españoleto★** and a crypt where the **tombs of the Dukes★** can be found. The **calle San Pedro★** has a number of historic buildings and churches, as well as the former university.

Punta Umbría
On the Atlantic coast 24km (15 miles) south of Huelva, known for its magnificent beach almost 20km (12 miles) long.

Mojácar, near Almería.

Skiers enjoy the Sierra Nevada.

Ronda la Vieja (N of Ronda)
A former Roman city, at an altitude of 1000m (3 280ft). There are only a few remains, including the theatre. There is a magnificent view of the Serranía de Ronda.

San Pedro de Alcántara
This is a new, or rather enlarged, town on the Costa del Sol, which is less spoiled than many of the others and handy for tours into the hinterland, such as the Serranía and Ronda. The **old centre** of San Pedro is very pleasant, with cobbled streets and plazas.

Sierra Nevada★★
This is the main winter sports area of Andulucia. It is also a centre for mountain walking and hiking. **Solynieve** ('Sun and Snow') is new and brash – the best ski resort in Spain, set on the high slopes of the Sierra Nevada, 32km (20 miles) from the city of Granada. In summer it is a walking centre, and the views from the Mulhacén peak extend on a good day to the shores of the Mediterranean or even across to North Africa.

Tarifa
Tarifa is not only a great **windsurfing centre** with a good beach, but has a fine **old town**, off the well-trodden tourist route but well worth visiting.

Torremolinos
Most of this stretch of coast, once

A quieter part of Torremolinos.

a series of windmill towers, has been transformed into a brash tourist resort, though a few remnants of the old town are left.

Ubrique
Ubrique is another shopping centre, set in the Serranía between Grazalema and Jimena de la Frontera, at the foot of a steep hillside. It is a **leather** centre (look for shoes, coats and handbags). Take a camera as well, for the setting is superb.

Vejer de la Frontera★
Picturesque hill town, with fine **views★** from its Moorish castle.

Zahara de los Atunes
Near Cádiz, the 'flower of the tuna fish', should be known for its wonderful unspoilt sandy beach, 9½km (6 miles) long.

Zuheros (SW of Córdoba)
A charming village with neat houses, sitting on the edge of a precipice. In most places you climb up to the fortress – here you climb down roughly-paved streets to get to it. In the heart of Sierra Subbética, it is favoured by hikers and hunters and has a pleasant rural hotel.

Vejer de la Frontera.

ENJOYING ANDALUCIA

To enjoy Andalucia you have to understand its pace: apart from bullfights, processions and the high speed train, punctuality is an unknown concept which, if it occurs, is completely by chance. It is hardly surprising that Andalucians are wild about fanciful artists, plunged deep into the inspiration of the moment: this is what their daily life is made of. Copy their daily rhythm, cut in two by a long siesta and with evenings which extend far into the night and long meal breaks. Share with them the wild fiestas to which they hold the secret. Whether for tourists or locals, all are treated with the greatest seriousness.

Watch the street show: the care with which these people decorate their towns; the noisy vitality around the numerous lottery ticket sellers shouting out their insistent *Para hoy!* to announce the daily draw (the ONCE, the association for the blind, has the monopoly of the lottery and is the most prosperous organisation in Spain); the indolence of the customers on the café terraces whilst a 'limpiabotas', with all his paraphernalia, busily shines the leather of their shoes (their colleagues in tourist areas insist on shining everything down to a pair of espadrilles); and the incessant flapping of fans, skilfully handled.

You may be surprised at the coexistence of an extremely modern society alongside traditional ways of life (tapas bars have served as a defence against fast food restaurants), fashionable boutiques alongside ancient stalls run by guilds which have elsewhere disappeared. And perhaps also the general hubbub of public places, for an Andalucian crowd expresses itself several decibels above its French equivalent. If you join in, you will be accepted – there is no need to master Spanish, if you have been seen three days in a row in the same café, you will be treated like one of the regulars!

WEATHER

The best months to visit Southern Spain are April and May, October and November. July and August can be very hot and it can rain heavily in early September. December and January evenings can be quite cold, though the days will be sunny and warm.

Snow falls on the Mulhacén peak and across the Sierra Nevada and lasts from late November to early May, but the weather in general tends to be sunny and warm. Temperatures rise to the 30s°C (80-90°F) during the summer months and fall to the mid- to upper-20s°C (65-75°F) in the winter.

Winter visitors will need a pullover, and a coat for evenings. Cotton clothing, suncream and a hat are suggested for the summer.

CALENDAR OF EVENTS

Southern Spain has two cultures, religion and tradition, and one or the other keeps the region busy with pilgrimages or fiestas throughout the year, with a concentration of events close to Christmas and Easter. Details of any local festivities can be obtained from the local tourist office. Do not be wary of attending; the local people will make you welcome.

The main events are as follows:

January
6 The Three Kings Festival on Twelfth Night. This is held all over Spain and is mainly for the children.

10-15 Pilgrimage of Torre García in Almería.

17 Festival of San Antón (St Anthony). Held all over Southern Spain.

February
Carnival before Ash Wednesday. All over the region but notably in Cádiz, with perhaps the most exciting carnival in Europe!

March-April
Holy Week in Seville. Processions, services, pilgrimages. Not an event to miss. Held also in Málaga, Jaén, Arcos de la Frontera, Baeza, Úbeda, Jerez and Puente Genil in Córdoba. At Baena, near Córdoba, a drum is beaten continuously for two days over Easter. Every town and almost every village in Southern Spain commemorates Holy Week.

April
The April Fair in Seville is held

The April Fair in Seville.

two weeks after Easter.

The pilgrimage to Our Lady of Cabeza, on the last Sunday in April at Andújar, is a splendid affair with riders and horse-drawn carriages.

May

The celebration of May Day, with songs and the erection of holy crosses draped with flowers, in or outside private homes. Especially in Córdoba and linked into the Spring Fiesta de los Patios, where courtyards are filled with flowers.

1-7 Jerez Horse Fair. Subject to equine fever restrictions and may be held at the end of April; check with the tourist boards.

Whitsun pilgrimage to the shrine of Our Lady at Rocío, near Almonte Huelva. The most famous pilgrimage in Spain after the one to Santiago de Compostela. Up to a million pilgrims and visitors, many on horseback or in carriages.

June

Corpus Christi. All over Spain, but in Andalucia especially in Granada (local feast and fair) and Seville where it is a holiday and where six boys dance before the altar in red costumes and then lead the procession, which includes *gigantes*, people wearing masks and giant papier-mâché heads. Also in Córdoba (procession on the following Sunday) and Zahara.

23 Eve of John the Baptist festivities with bonfires in Vispera de San Juan.

24 Fair of John the Baptist. At Cádiz the summer solstice is also celebrated.

The colourful Jerez Horse Fair is held in May.

July

25 Fiesta of St James (Santiago) of Compostela, the patron saint of Spain, celebrated all over Southern Spain but especially in Granada, the Alpujarras villages, Jaén and Cádiz

August

5 Pilgrimage of the Virgin of Nieves at Trevélez (Granada). The pilgrimage ascends the peak of the Mulhacén.

15 The Assumption. A public holiday in Spain and a big religious festival.

18-21 Fiesta del Guadalquivir at Sanlúcar de Barrameda.

September

6 Annual encounter between the

men of Guadiz and Baza (Granada). A good-humoured brawl for the right to hold the statue of the Virgin of Piety.

7-14 Moscatel Fiesta, Chipiona. A gypsy festival well known for first-class flamenco.

Wine festival and Harvest Fair, at Palma del Condado, held at various dates in September.

October

3 Sunday Virgin del Valme pilgrimage at Seville.

7 Fiesta of the Virgin of the Rosario at Mojácar.

19 Fiesta of San Pedro de Alcántara (Town).

24 Festival of St Raphael celebrated in Córdoba.

November

1 All Saints Day. Family festival and fiestas.

2 All Souls Day. Visits to family graves; day of remembrance.

December

25 Nativity; Christmas Day.

28 Day of the Holy Innocents; some churches elect a Boy Bishop.

31 Bonfire Festival at Huesa (Jaén).

31 New Year's Eve. The Spanish tradition is to pop a grape into your mouth at each stroke of midnight and try to swallow the lot before the last chime. Those who succeed will enjoy a lot of luck in the coming year – but it isn't easy!

ACCOMMODATION

See also p.106 for more details.
Those on a tight budget will find a place to stay for a modest price in the centre of Seville (Calle Archeros in particular), Córdoba or Granada in boarding houses or small hotels sometimes indicated by the word *camas* (beds): spartan, and breakfast unknown but the rooms sometimes open onto charming courtyards.

The Association of Rural Andalucian Hotels incorporates some 30 establishments. You can obtain the list from **AHRA**, c/Obispo Cobos 2, Centro Cultural Hospital de Santiago, 23400 Úbeda (Jaén) ☎ **953 75 58 67**, fax 953 75 60 99. A voucher system enables you to pay half the price when you book (the remainder being paid directly to the hotel). But reservations are made direct with each hotel.

Some hotel addresses:
In **Granada**, in the Alhambra, the small hotel **América** ☎ **958 22 74 71**, a marvellous setting for a dream visit. But the **Alhambra Palace** remains a must, in a curious neo-Arab building built in 1911 ☎ **958 22 14 68**. In town, you will find several comfortable and well situated hotels, such as the **Triunfo Granada** ☎ **958 20 74 44**, **Dauro II** ☎ **958 22 15 81**, and the **Navas** ☎ **958 22 59 59**.

In **Seville** a favourite is **las Casas**

Matadores at a bull fight.

de la Judería ☎ **954 41 50 50**, a stone's throw from Santa Cruz: courtyards, a maze of corridors (get someone to help guide the car out onto the street). The hotel **Alfonso XIII** ☎ **954 22 28 50** may seduce enthusiasts with its outdated luxury. The **Gran Hotel Lar** ☎ **954 41 03 61**, modern and comfortable, is well situated. You may choose to sleep outside the city; why not in **Carmona** in the marvellous **Hotel Casa de Carmona** ☎ **954 19 10 00**, tastefully decorated in original style, with dining room in the former stables.

In **Córdoba**, opposite the Mezquita, is the hotel **El**

Conquistador ☎ 957 48 11 02. In the streets of old Córdoba, the hotel **Albucasis** ☎ 957 47 86 25 is full of charm. The **Alfaros** hotel ☎ 957 49 19 20 must also be mentioned and, more modest, the **Hotel Maestre** ☎ 957 47 24 10, near to the plazuela del Potro. But it can be difficult to reach them by car. You may prefer to stay outside the city (to the north), where several hotels offer vast gardens with swimming pools and tennis courts. Some 60kms (37 miles) to the south, the rural hotel **Zuhayra** ☎ 957 69 46 93, in the village of

Zuheros, is the ideal place for a visit to Subbética Mountain Park.

In **Ronda**, the hotel **Reina Victoria** ☎ 952 87 12 40 has a lovely garden with views of the Tajo.

Other Andalucian hotels worth a visit for their charm or setting – even just for a drink – include the **Parador de Arcos de la Frontera** (Plaza del Cabildo ☎ 956 70 05 00), the **Parador de Málaga**, located on Gibralfaro Hill (☎ 952 22 19 02), the **Parador de Jaén**, set inside a 13C fortress (☎ 953 23 00 00) and the **Parador de Úbeda** (Plaza Vázquez Molina ☎ 953 75 03 45), in

A ceramic shop in Ronda.

a 16C palace. For those who dream of living the life of an Andalucian *señorito* for a day or two, there is the **Hacienda Benazuza**, situated inside a superbly restored Arab-Andalucian building in **Sanlúcar la Mayor**, a few kilometres from Seville (☎ 955 70 33 44).

FOOD AND DRINK

The food of Andalucia is a wonderful blend of Arab, Jewish, Mediterranean and other influences. The midday heat – and very necessary siesta – means the day begins early and runs late, with lunch around 2pm or 3pm and dinner never before 9pm or 10pm. To fill the gap the Spanish invented *tapas*, a vast selection of snacks:

tortilla slices, *calamares*, olives, anchovies, and anything that comes in small portions. Ask for a *porción*, or a *ración*, if you want a larger helping.

A typical meal begins with an aperitif beer, then perhaps the superb but expensive baked ham (*jamón serrano*). You may like one of the many variants of the cold soup (*gazpacho*). In Córdoba, bread, oil, tomato and garlic make *salmorejo*; in Antequera there is a red pepper version and you may find one made with almonds. Seafood is plentiful and excellent. For a special occasion have the saffron-scented rice dish *paella*. With this drink a light dry *fino* sherry, the exquisite *manzanilla*, from Jerez, Montilla or

Sanlúcar.

In Andalucia the poultry and meat are also good. Look for the traditional *rabo de toro*, bull's tail. With this you should drink the red wines of Rioja or Valdepenas, or ask for bottled water which comes with or without bubbles (*con gas*, or *sin gas*). It is possible to eat very cheaply in the large restaurants which, in the immediate vicinity of tourist attractions, offer '*platos combinados*'. But the quality is in keeping with the price. Fish lovers (especially of *pescaítos fritos*) should try the '*chiringuitos*', near beaches.

Some restaurant suggestions:
In Córdoba
El Churrasco *Romero 16*, a stone's

The elegant resort of Puerto Banús.

throw from the mosque. Bodega and restaurant in a covered courtyard. Grilled pork (*churrasco*) a speciality but you can taste Córdoban cuisine in general here. Nearby, **El Caballo Rojo** *Cardenal Herreros 28*, is also well-known and, near to the Alcázar, **Almudaina** *Jardines de los Santos Mártires 1*, in a particularly nice setting.

In Granada
Chikito *Puerta Real*, in memory of Lorca. **Pilar del Toro** *Santa Ana 12*, an immense courtyard full of huge tables and a maze of rooms upstairs. Not easy to find. In the Albaícin, the **Casa Torcuato** *Plaza de Carniceros*, is a simple and pleasant restaurant run by a flamenco enthusiast: specialities of Granada etc.

Finally, in the lower part of town, **Mariquilla** *Lope de Vega 2*, offers good value for money, while **Cunini** *Plaza Pescadería*, not far from the cathedral, is a favourite with seafood-lovers.

In Seville
La Taberna del Alabardero *Zaragoza 20*, dining room on the first floor around the courtyard of a former stately home with sophisticated food. In the corner of the Alcázar gardens, opposite the University, **Egaña Oriza** *San Fernando 41*, good cuisine in a winter garden.
El Burladero *Canalejas 1*, underneath the hotel Colón: the

rendezvous of the bullfighting world during festivals.

In Santa Cruz, try the charm of a candlelit dinner in a tree filled courtyard at **El Corral del Agua** *c/Agua 6*, and on the plaza Santa Cruz, **La Albahaca**, located in a stately home.

Most of the Paradors offer regional specialities and the price is no higher than elsewhere.

Other places
In **Ronda**, **Tragabuches** *Aparicio 1, near the Plaza de Toros*, honours the memory of an amazing *rondeño* who was a brilliant *torero* and bloodthirsty bandit. Nowadays, it is a very trendy spot.
In **Arcos de la Frontera**, the hotel **El Convento** restaurant, situated on an Andalucian patio, has an excellent choice of local dishes.
In **Sanlúcar de Barrameda**, **Casa Bigote** (on the fishing port) has been the favourite haunt of shellfish-lovers for half a century. Establishments offering good food at decent prices can also be found in **Almería** (**Veracruz**, *Av del Cabo de Gata*), **Cazorla** (**La Sarga**, *Plaza del Mercado*), **Almuñecar** (**Mar de Plata**, *Paseo San Cristóbal*) and **San Fernando**, near Cadiz (**Venta los Tarantos**, *Cuesta de la Ardila 53*).

SHOPPING

The best buys in Southern Spain come from the local craftsmen. Córdoba is famous for its leather workers and **Córdovan leather** is superb, so this is the place to buy shoes or handbags or leather coats. Another good buy in Córdoba is the **filigree silverware**, which can be found in craft shops and workshops all over the Judería, especially in the Calle de los Flores, near the Mezquita. La Rambla, 30 km (18 miles) from Córdoba has around 100 pottery workshops selling many types of pottery including the famous **Caliphal ceramics**.

Woollens, linens, sherry wines and olive oil are also superb and not expensive if you shop away from the tourist areas. The main streets of Córdoba, Seville, Granada and Jaén have plenty of fashionable shops and the **Fajalauza ware** of Granada is widely available in the shops of the Albaicín.

Southern Spain is also a good place to buy sports clothing and equipment for tennis, golf, windsurfing or sailing, especially at the end of season. In the country districts many towns and villages have an *artesanía*, a centre for selling locally produced craft goods, including garments like ponchos and *jarapas*.

ENTERTAINMENT AND NIGHTLIFE

If you want to discover bullfighting, it is best to do so during the Seville April Fair or at the **goyesque bullfights** in Ronda in September (but tickets are

Gazpacho – a cold cucumber and tomato soup.

difficult to obtain). Failing this, visit during another *feria* such as those in Jérez, Córdoba, Granada, Málaga or Almería or in towns like Puerto de Santa María, Sanlúcar de Barrameda, Antequera or Écija, where bullfighting is fully appreciated. Avoid the bullrings of the seaside resorts, even if big names are advertised: the stars come here mainly chasing work. Remember that a bullfight **always** starts at the advertised time. The price of tickets depends on how far the seat is from the ring, but also its position in relation to the sun: *sol*, *sol y sombra* and *sombra*.

It is difficult to say where you should go to see a good **flamenco** show. The Sacromonte clubs in Granada and the **tablaos** of the Costa del Sol are largely tourist traps. Try those in Seville or the more serious ones of Jérez. Or take advantage of the many festivals which are held in Seville, Córdoba, Jérez and Granada.

Cabaret, night club and discotheque enthusiasts are spoilt for choice in the Costa del Sol resorts, where huge rock concerts are held in summer.

Nights during a fiesta go on well into the early hours. Dusk marks the start of the *paseo* (evening stroll), accompanied by a round of the bars: the **tapeo** is methodically undertaken and enables Andalucian gastronomy to be discovered thanks to *tapas*. This is a great way of tasting the region's specialities!

SPORTS AND PASTIMES

The great modern sport of Southern Spain is **golf**. The Costa del Sol in particular has dozens of championship golf courses, which attract both professionals and amateurs from all over the world. The second most popular sport is **tennis**, with hundreds of courts in tourist resorts, holiday hotels and in a growing number of tennis ranches run by professionals.

Watersports are equally well catered for. There are plenty of marinas and every beach has at least one windsurfing and sailing school, with sailboards or dinghies for hire, though a certificate of

The beautiful golf course at Torrequebrada, near Málaga.

competence will be needed or tuition insisted upon. The great mecca for windsurfers is Tarifa, near Cádiz, where the strong winds and currents call for a degree of skill and experience.

Behind the Costas there is great scope for **rural pursuits**: horse riding, pony trekking, even mule trekking from villages in the Sierra Nevada and the Alpujarras. Tuition is usually available. Walking in high summer can be a testing experience and the hills are both rugged, remote and not well waymarked. The climb to the Mulhacén from Sol y Nieve is a good excursion and there is good walking into the Serranía de Ronda from Jimenez de la Frontera and many of the White or Frontera towns. Wise walkers will wear boots, and carry a map, a compass and a bottle of water.

The best windsurfing in Southern Spain is reputedly at Tarifa.

Skiing is also popular, with Sol y Nieve, near Granada, being one of the best resorts in Spain, with slopes tough enough to take the resort onto the World Cup circuit. The season runs from late November to the end of April; sometimes it is possible to ski on the Valeta slopes in the morning and swim in the sea in the afternoon.

There is also great scope for **exploring wildlife** and **birdwatching**. The great variety of terrain produces a wide range of plantlife and an abundance of wildlife, including deer and wild boar. The main centre for birders is the **Doñana National Park ☎ 959 43 04 32/43 04 51** (*see also* p.48).

Apart from the Doñana National Park there are **nature reserves** or **mountain parks** at Las Marismas del Odiel, south-west of Huelva; at Córdoba Lagunas; in the Sierra de Grazalema; in the Sierras de Cazorla and Segura near Jaén and in the Trocal de Antequera, in the province of Málaga. The Sierra de Hornachuelos is known for its numerous birds of prey; the Sierra Mágina for its craggy scenery and ibex among the olive trees, and Los Alcornocales for cork oak, the last remaining example of primitive European forest.

Marine parks can be found at Cabo de gata/Níjar which has a bird observatory, a naturalist centre at El Bujo and viewpoints. Other marine parks inlcude those at Marismas de Barbate and Bahia de Cádiz.

Also the largest saline lake in Andalucia is at Lago de la Fuente de Piedra, north-west of Antequera. This has the largest colony in Europe of Greater Flamingoes. Wildlife lovers with lots of patience can expect to see mountain goats, boar and even lynx, in some of these Andalucian reserves. Full details can be obtained from the local tourist offices.

Rugged terrain of the Sierra de Almijara, near Nerja.

THE BASICS

Before you Go

Visitors entering Spain should have a full passport, valid to cover the period in which they will be travelling. No visa is required for members of EU countries or US, Canadian or New Zealand citizens, but visitors from Australia do require a visa, which can be obtained on arrival for a period of up to 30 days.

No vaccinations are necessary.

Getting There
By Air

The two international airports at Seville and Málaga serve the region of Andalucia. You can also land at Granada, Almería or Jerez, changing at Madrid.

Charter flights usually offer the best price deal, although return times are fixed so that the maximum time you can spend in Spain is four weeks. Package holidays offer great value too, and sometimes the price is so reasonable that you can buy a holiday to an unpopular resort just for the flight, and still afford to stay in the place of your choice.

There are also numerous scheduled flights to Spain from all over the world. Those coming from the US will probably fly directly to Madrid, with connections to either Málaga or Seville laid on, though sometimes it is cheaper to fly to London first, or another European city, before getting a connecting flight to Spain. The superfast trains – the AVE and the Talgo – connect Madrid with Córdoba, Seville and Málaga.

Direct charter flights go from Dublin and Belfast to Málaga during the summer months, and scheduled flights leave all year round for Madrid.

Lovely Spanish villages such as Mojácar are found all around Southern Spain.

Visitors from Australia and New Zealand cannot get a direct flight to Spain, but will have to make a stopover at another European city before being able to take a connecting flight on to Andalucia.

Low-cost flights from any-where in the world can be arranged through flight agents or by booking a charter flight, and APEX or super-APEX tickets may be bought directly from the airlines. The travel advertisements in the English weekend newspapers or the various London listing magazines are the best places for travellers from the UK to look. Travel clubs and discount agents offer good savings from North America and Australasia.

By Train
The journey by train from London to Málaga, changing at Paris and Barcelona, takes about 35 hours using Eurostar and the Channel Tunnel. There are various rail passes which offer substantial discounts on rail travel, particularly if you are planning a journey throughout Europe. Details are obtainable from Rail Europe in New York (☎ 800 438 7245), or Rail Europe in London (☎ 0990 848 848).

By Coach
Buses leave London for Barcelona, Alicante, Algeciras and Madrid several times a week, and journey times are tediously long, so a stopover inside the Spanish border is recommended.

By Ferry
There are various options for those wanting to take their own car to Southern Spain. Two ferries companies offer direct sailings to Bilbao and Santander from Britain: Brittany Ferries and P&O European Ferries. The advantage of this crossing is that the long – and expensive – drive through France is completely eliminated. If you do plan to drive through France, one of the fastest routes is by Le Shuttle, which runs from Folkestone via the Channel Tunnel to France in 35 minutes; this service for cars continues 24 hours a day throughout the year.

Several ferry companies carry cars and passengers across the Channel, with the quickest journeys being between Dover/Calais, and Folkestone/Boulogne. The hovercraft is even faster, crossing from Dover to Calais in just 35 minutes. Brittany Ferries offer crossings from Portsmouth, Plymouth and Poole directly to Brittany, arriving at St Malo and Roscoff.

A-Z

Accidents and Breakdowns

If you are involved in an accident while driving in Spain you should exchange full details of insurance, addresses, etc. See also information about bail bonds under **Driving**. In an emergency, ☎ **091** or for the Road Helpline ☎ **900 12 35 03**.

Accommodation

Accommodation in Spain ranges from simple to luxurious, and with prices to match. The *Michelin Red Guide Spain and Portugal* lists a selection of hotels. Prices vary with demand, and increase considerably at times of popular feasts, such as Easter in Seville.

Fondas offer the most basic form of accommodation, and can be identified by a square blue sign with a white 'F' in it. They are often sited above a bar. Next come *casas de huéspedes* (CH on a similar background), *pensiones* (P), and *hospedajes*.

More common than these four simple types of accommodation are *hostales* (marked Hs) and *hostal-residencias* (HsR), both ranging from one to three stars and offering good en-suite or private facilities.

Hoteles (H) are graded from one to five stars, with a one-star hotel costing about the same as three-star *hostales*.

Details of **youth hostels** are provided by TIVE, José Ortega y Gasset 71, 28006 Madrid; ☎ **913 47 77 78**. Andalucia has a network of 18 youth hostels mainly in the larger towns and beach resorts. To obtain a bed, you must have a card (group or individual) which can be obtained in the Hostels or from the central reservation department of **Inturjoven**: c/Miño, 24, 41011 Seville ☎ **954 55 82 93**, fax 954 55 82 92.

For a more rural stay the **Villas Turisticas** (3 stars) have six hotels in Andalucia. Contact Asociacion de Hoteles Rurales de Andalucia, c/Jose Zorilla 5, 14008 Córdoba ☎ (& fax) **957 49 04 18**. Also Farm and Country Homes offer accommodation at farms and in local homes. Further information from Red Andaluza de Alojamientos Rurales, Apartado de Correos 2035, 04080 Almería ☎ 950 26 58 18, fax 950 27 04 31.

There are a few self-catering cottages in Andalucia. For a list of them, consult the following web sites: www.ruralia.es and www.agrotur.com.

Mountain areas offer *refugios*: basic dormitory huts with cheap shelter for hikers or climbers. Information from the Federación Española de Montañismo, Calla Alberto Aguilera 3, 28015 Madrid; ☎ 914 45 13 82.
See **Paradors p.121** *and also* **Accommodation p.94**

Banks
Banks are open 8.30am-2pm, Monday to Friday. Main branches are also open on Saturday from 9am-12.30/1pm. Between June and September banks are closed on Saturday.

Most major credit cards are widely accepted but cash may be needed in the smaller villages. Alliance & Leicester Giro operates an international cash card system which allows cash withdrawals on personal UK bank accounts. For details contact Alliance & Leicester Giro at Bootle, Merseyside GIR

OAA; ☎ 0645 250 250.

Eurocheques backed up by a Eurocheque card, and drawn on bank accounts in most European countries, can be used in banks, and to pay for goods in hotels, restaurants and shops. Most cheque cards, and Visa and Mastercard, can be used to withdraw cash from automatic cash machines.

Banks will usually change travellers' cheques, but charge high rates, and there are also specialist exchange bureaux. Exchange facilities at El Corte Inglés, a department store found throughout Spain, offer competitive rates.

Bicycles
Cycling is a cheap and popular way of getting about in Spain, although Andalucia is quite mountainous, and summer

Tourism takes over at Torremolinos.

temperatures are very high.

Motorists usually hoot before they pass a cyclist, and this acts as a useful early-warning system. Be aware that helmet wearing is compulsory on bicycles.

Bodegas

This is where the wines are matured (in Jérez, Sanlúcar etc.) but it is also the name for places where wine is drunk. A great place for *tapas* and *fino*. To help choose, follow the 'movida'. The most traditional are worth visiting for their setting: walls covered in ceramic tiles, barrels, whole hams hung from hooks, etc.

In **Seville**, in the El Arenal district (around the bullring, plaza del Salvador (under the porticos, the *Los Soportales* bar), opposite the cathedral, calle Rodrigo Caro (*Las Columnas*), near to Sierpes (calle Góngora), in the Santa Cruz district and, some distance from the town centre, the picturesque *Riconcillo* (c/Gerona 20) unchanged since 1670. One regular client is immortalised there in ceramic tiles as a celebration of

A beautiful sandy beach, one of many to be found on the Costa de la Luz.

50 years of loyalty.

In **Granada**, on the Campo del Príncipe; in the calle Navas; around the Plaza Nueva which has the magnificent *bodega Castañeda.*

In **Córdoba**, in the Judería and under the archways of the Corredera.

Books

A visit to any region is more enjoyable if you know a bit about it, and there are a surprising number of books available, and in English, about life in Andalucia. Here are some suggestions:

Gerald Brenan's *South from Granada* concerns his life in Alhaurín and the Alpujarras in the years between the two world wars and during the Spanish Civil War. *The Spanish Labyrinth,* is a clear evocation of the Spanish Civil War of 1936-1939 and the rise to power of General Franco.

Hugh Thomas's *The Spanish Civil War* is a more detailed story from a historian.

Nicholas Luard's *Andalucía* is useful to wildlife enthusiasts.

Robin Totton's *Andalucía* is extremely entertaining as a general guide.

Richard Ford's idiosyncratic *Handbook for a Traveller in Spain* written in 1845 is a wonderful book, now out of print, but available from public libraries.

Penelope Chetwode's *Two Middle Aged Ladies in Andalucía,* for those who like getting off the beaten track – especially as one of the 'ladies' is a mule.

In Moguer de la Frontera, you should read *Platero and I*, by the well-known writer Juan Ramón Jiménez, considered to be a master by the poets from the 1927 generation.

References to contemporary

Andalucia can also be found in some of the novels by Antonio Muñoz Molina (from Jaén). Bullfighting fans will want to read two works by Hemingway: *Death in the Afternoon* and *The Dangerous Summer* (the latter is about Ordóñez, the famous *torero* from Ronda).

Camping

There are over 100 authorized campsites in Andalucia, most of them along the coast. The most beautifully sited and best equipped charge the highest rates. For a free list of these sites, contact the Spanish National Tourist Office in your own country, *see* **Tourist Information Offices**).

Unauthorized camping is not recommended, and though you might just get moved on by the authorities, you may be unlucky.

For particular information on Spanish campsites or making a booking, contact the site directly, or Federación Española de Empresarios de Campings y C.V. General Oraa, 52–2°D 28006 Madrid; ☎ **915 62 99 94**.

Car Hire

Car hire in Southern Spain is among the cheapest in Europe,

The arid inland landscape covered with thousands of olive trees, near Jaén.

and Andalucia is well stocked with car hire agencies; there are outlets at airports, air terminals and the major railway stations, as well as at large hotels. Airlines and tour operators offer fly/drive arrangements, which can be very good value, although you will also get a good deal if you hire from a small local firm. Make sure that collision damage waiver is included in the insurance.

The lower age limit is 21, but few international companies hire to drivers under 23, or even 25. Drivers must have held their full licence for at least a year.

With the exception of Avis, there is an upper age limit of 60-65. Unless paying by credit card a substantial cash deposit is required, but full details of the different hire schemes can be obtained from tourist offices. If you are driving a car that has obviously been hired, take extra precautions when parking, and never leave anything of value inside.
See also **Accidents and Breakdowns**, and **Tourist Information Offices.**

Clothing
Comfortable casual clothing is ideal when holidaying in Spain, with the emphasis on beachwear

The church at Estepona on the Costa del Sol.

for days by the coast. Hats are vital for those who venture out in the midday sun, and children should always wear a hat in the soaring summer temperatures.

The people living in the countryside of Southern Spain tend to be quite conservative, and whilst topless sunbathing is a fact of life by the sea, it is advisable to dress discreetly in towns and rural areas.

Complaints
Complaints about goods or services should ideally be made at the time, in a quiet and calm manner. At a restaurant or hotel make your complaint to the manager.

All hotels, restaurants, camp sites and petrol stations are required by law to keep and produce complaint forms when required by a customer to do so. If this proves to be difficult to achieve, ask the local tourist information office to intervene on your behalf (*see* **Tourist Information Offices**).

Consulates
Many countries have consulates and consular agents in Andalucia, while embassies tend to be based in Madrid.

British Consulates:
Málaga ☎ 952 21 75 71.
Seville ☎ 954 22 88 75.
US Consulates:
Seville ☎ 954 23 18 85.
Fuengirola☎ 952 47 98 91.
Canadian Consulates:
Málaga ☎ 952 22 33 46.
Seville ☎ 954 22 94 13.
Irish Consulates:
Málaga ☎ 952 47 51 08.
Seville ☎ 954 21 63 61.

Crime

To avoid pickpockets, the best advice is to be aware at all times, carry as little money, and as few credit cards as possible, and leave any valuables in the hotel safe.

Carry wallets and purses in secure pockets inside your outer clothing, wear body belts, or carry handbags across your body or firmly under your arm.

Never leave your car unlocked, and hide away or remove items of value. Theft of cars or their contents is particularly bad in cities like Seville and Málaga, and you are advised to remove any evidence that your car has been hired, as thieves are attracted to them in particular. If you have anything stolen, report it immediately to the nearest police station or police office – *Centro Atencíon Policial* – where English-speaking officers can offer practical advice. Collect a report so that you can make an insurance claim. If your passport is stolen, report it to the Consulate or Embassy at once.

Customs and Entry Regulations

There is no limit on the importation into Spain of tax-paid goods bought in an EU country provided they are for personal consumption, with the exception of alcohol and tobacco which have fixed limits governing them.

Disabled Visitors

Spain is not the most accessible country for disabled travellers, and public transport is particularly difficult for wheelchairs. The *Michelin Red Guide España-Portugal* indicates which hotels have facilities for the disabled.

In Britain, RADAR, at 12 City Forum, 250 City Road, London EC1V 8AF; ☎ 020 7250 3222, publishes fact sheets, and a guide to facilities and accommodation overseas for the disabled visitor.

The Spanish National Tourist Office in your own country is a good source of information. You are also advised to check with hotels and travel agents to see that your individual needs can be met.

Driving

Drivers should carry a full national or international driving licence, insurance documents, including a green card (no longer compulsory for EU members but strongly recommended), registration papers for the car, and a nationality sticker for the car rear. You must also have two warning triangles for use in the event of a breakdown.

A bail bond or extra insurance cover for legal costs is also worth investing in, since as a foreigner you may be blamed for any accident you are in, regardless of who is really at fault. Without a bail bond, the car could be impounded and the driver placed under arrest.

The minimum age for driving is 18, and cars drive on the right. Away from main roads cars give way to those approaching from the right. Front seat passengers must wear seatbelts outside of urban areas.

Speed limits are as follows:
Maximum on urban roads: 60kph/37mph
Maximum on other roads: 90kph or 100kph/56 or 62mph
Dual carriageways: 120kph/75mph.
Speed traps are used, and if you are stopped for speeding, the police are likely to impose a hefty on-the-spot fine. Also note that Spanish motorways have tolls.

Electric Current
The voltage in Spain is usually 220 or 225V. Plugs and sockets are of the two-pin variety, and adaptors are generally required. North Americans will probably also need a transformer.

Emergencies
In an emergency, contact the police or your consulate who will offer very limited help. The universal emergency telephone number is ☎ 091.

Etiquette
As in most places in the world, you should dress respectfully in churches and museums. Be sensitive to conservative attitudes away from the cities and resorts.

Excursions
Andalucia is one of the most beautiful places in the world, and as well as its incredible natural wonders, it is packed with castles, Moorish monuments and Gothic cathedrals.

In addition to these sights, there is usually a festival in some tiny village or small town which is great fun to attend.

Explore the amazing landscape of the Riotinto open-air mines on board the **Ferrocarril Turístico-minero**, a

Calahonda beach at Nerja.

Spanish cathedrals and churches are full of intricate carvings and designs. This one is at Ubeda.

venerable railway that still uses tracks built in the 19C by the mining company.

The Adriano III **ferry** makes the crossing between Puerto Santa María and Cadiz in 40 minutes. The lower Guadalquivir Valley and Doñana National Park between Seville and Sanlúcar can also be explored by boat with **Cruceros turísticos por el Gualdalquivir**. Boats leave across from the Torre de Oro in Seville.

Epicureans may wish to explore Andalucia aboard a moving palace, the **Al Andalus Expreso**, which features a six-night trip from Madrid to Seville, with stopovers in Grenada, Carmona, Ronda or Jérez.

Health

UK nationals should carry a Form E111 (forms available from post offices) which is produced by the Department of Health, and which entitles the holder to free urgent treatment for accident or illness in EU countries. The treatment will have to be paid for in the first instance, but can be reclaimed later. All foreign nationals, including those from the UK, are advised to take out comprehensive insurance cover, and to keep any bills, receipts and invoices to support any claim.

Lists of doctors can be obtained from hotels, chemists or the local consulate, and first aid and medical advice is also available at the *farmacia*, from pharmacists who are highly trained and can dispense drugs which are available only on prescription in other countries.

The *farmacia* is open from 9/10am-1.30pm, closes for lunch at 1.30/2pm and then reopens at 4.30pm until about 8pm. Those which are open late or on Sundays display notices on their doors, and on the doors of other pharmacies.

You can get the address of an English-speaking doctor from your consulate, the police station, the *farmacia* or the tourist office.

Language

English is spoken widely in the main tourist areas, but elsewhere you will be grateful for any little bit of Spanish that you have learned. In any case, your efforts to speak Spanish will be much appreciated everywhere, and even a few simple words and expressions are often warmly received.

Below are a few words and phrases that will help you make the most of your stay in Spain.

Yes/no	*Sí/no*
Please/thank you	*Por favor/gracias*
Do you speak English?	*¿Habla (usted) inglés?*
How much is it?	*¿Cuánto es?*
Excuse me	*Perdone*
I'd like a stamp	*Quisiera un sello*
How are you?	*¿Cómo está (usted)?*
I don't understand	*No entiendo*
See you later	*Hasta luego*
Do you have a room?	*¿Tiene una habitación?*
How do I get to ....?	*¿Por dónde se va a...?*

Lost Property

Airports and major railway stations have their own lost property offices, and if something goes missing in your hotel, check with the hotel reception. Report all lost or stolen items to the police, and always be sure to get a report to substantiate any insurance claims, but don't expect the police to get too excited about minor thefts.

Should you lose any travel documents, contact the police, and in the event of a passport going missing, inform your Embassy or Consulate immediately (*see* **Consulates**).

Lost or stolen travellers' cheques and credit cards should be reported immediately to the issuing company with a list of numbers, and the police should also be informed.

Maps

There are a range of Michelin road atlases and sheet maps that cover Southern Spain. The spiral-bound *Michelin Road Atlas: Spain and Portugal* covers the whole of the Iberian peninsula. *Sheet map 446: Southern Spain* provides a detailed coverage of the region. Also available is the *Green Guide Spain* which describes many of the towns and villages in Southern Spain.

Hiking maps can be ordered from: Servicio de Publicaciones del Instituto Geográfico Nacional, General Ibáñez de Ibero, 28003, Madrid.

Michelin on-line:

Web surfers now have free access to 11 Michelin sites around the world (click 'Plan Your Route'), as well as the site www.michelin-travel.com. Itineraries can be planned using a database covering 26 countries and 1 500 000km of road networks, showing tolls, traffic conditions, mileage, estimated travelling times and digital maps for any trip over 50km. Based on the 12 books in the *Red Guide* series, the hotel and restaurant guide helps you to choose stopover points.

Money

The Spanish unit of currency is the peseta, with notes in denominations of 1 000, 2 000, 5 000 and 10 000 pesetas, and coins of 1, 5, 10, 25, 50, 100, 200 and 500 pesetas.

There is no restriction on bringing into or out of the country currency below the level of one million pesetas, but perhaps the safest way to carry large amounts of money is in travellers' cheques, which

are widely accepted and exchanged. Bureaux de change are found at airports, terminals and larger railway stations, and at banks (*see also* **Banks**).

On 1 January 1999 the **euro** became the official common currency in 11 countries, including Spain. Bank notes and coins will be introduced in all 11 countries on 1 January 2002. From then on, it will no longer be necessary to change money when travelling in the euro-zone countries.

The following chart will help you to calculate equivalencies between the peseta and the euro (1 euro = 166.39pts).

pts	euro	euro	pts
200	1.20	1	166.39
300	1.80	3	499.17
500	3.01	5	831.95
1 000	6.01	7	1 164.73
1 300	7.81	10	1 663.90
1 500	9.02	11	1 830.29

Newspapers

There are several English publications in Southern Spain, aimed at the large expat market and varying between decent glossies like *Lookout* which takes a serious look at Spanish affairs, and news sheets such as *The Marbella Times.*

British and other foreign newspapers are on sale in most cities and resorts, and the

Buying souvenirs in Torremolinos.

International Herald Tribune, published in Paris, offers the latest stock market news from America as well as world news.

Opening Hours

Shops in Spain are normally closed from 1.30pm-5/5.30pm. General stores open from 9/10am, close for lunch at 1.30/2pm and then reopen at 4.30/5pm until 8pm. Once or twice a week most Spanish towns and holiday resorts hold an open-air market, and details of these can be obtained locally.

Chemists are usually open the same times as shops, but some are open for longer hours and on Sundays, and there is usually a rota of chemists open for 24 hours (*see also* **Health**).

Monuments and museums tend to open between 10am-1pm and 4pm-7pm with several variations, while many churches only open for the early morning or evening service each day. *See also* **Banks** and **Post Offices**.

Paradors

Run by the State, Paradors are sometimes located in stately homes and sometimes in modern buildings with an exceptional location.

There are some 16 in Andalucia. The one in Granada, located in a former monastery within the grounds of the Alhambra, is the best known but those of Arcos de la Frontera, Úbeda and Carmona are equally exceptional. The Parador in Cádiz opens onto the ocean and in Málaga, from the top of the Gibralfaro hill, you will have an extremely beautiful view over the bay, whilst in Ronda a terrace and gardens give a view over the Tajo opposite the Puente Nuevo.

Reservations: Club Azur, 4 rue de Faubourg Montmartre, 75009 Paris ☎ 01 53 34 40 14/15, fax 01 53 34 40 16 and in Spain, Requena 3, 28013 Madrid ☎ 915 16 66 66, fax 91 516 66 57.

Andalucian Paradors:
Antequera ☎ 952 84 09 21
Arcos ☎ 956 70 05 00
Ayamonte ☎ 959 32 07 00

Cádiz ☎ 956 22 69 05
Carmona ☎ 954 14 10 10
Cazorla ☎ 953 72 70 75
Córdoba ☎ 957 27 59 00
Granada ☎ 958 22 14 40
Jaén ☎ 953 23 00 00
Málaga ☎ 952 22 19 02
Mazagón ☎ 959 53 63 00
Mojácar ☎ 950 47 82 50
Nerja ☎ 952 52 00 50
Ronda ☎ 952 87 75 00
Úbeda ☎ 953 75 03 45

Paradors are indicated on Michelin map 446 by the letter P on a yellow background.

Police

There are three types of police: the *Guardia Civil*, who wear green uniforms; the *Policía Municipal*, who wear blue and white uniforms with red trim and are generally sympathetic to tourists with genuine problems; and the *Policía Nacional*, who wear dark blue uniforms.

The national emergency telephone number for the Police is ☎ 091; the local emergency telephone number is ☎ 092 and the Guardia Civil (rural police) is ☎ 062.

Post Offices

Called *Correos*, these are open 8am-noon and 5pm-7.30pm in smaller towns, while those in cities and at airports are open for longer hours. Stamps are also available from tobacco shops (*estancos*).

Poste restante mail should be sent to the person (surname underlined) at Lista de Correos, followed by the town and province. Take a passport along as proof of identity when collecting mail.

British visitors can withdraw cash on their UK accounts with a National Girobank post-cheque (*see* **Banks**).

Public Holidays

New Year's Day: 1 January
Epiphany: 6 January
Andalucia National day:
    28 February
Good Friday (Easter Monday is not a holiday in Andalucia)
Labour Day: 1 May
Corpus Christi: 2nd Thursday after Whitsun(Granada/Seville)
Assumption Day: 15 August
National Day: 12 October
All Saints' Day: 1 November
Constitution Day: 6 December
Immaculate Conception:
    8 December
Christmas Day: 25 December
    There are also other feasts and public holidays which are celebrated locally, when almost everything shuts down.

Telephones

International telephone calls may be made from all Spanish provincial capital towns and most major holiday resorts.

Dial 07, wait for the dialling tone, and then dial the appropriate country code (44 for the UK, 353 for Eire, 1 for USA and Canada, 61 for Australia and 64 for New Zealand).

Spanish telephones have instructions in English, and take 5, 25 or 100 peseta coins, or phonecards of 1000 or 2000 pesetas which can be bought in tobacconists. International calls may be made in either telephone booths, or at a *Telefónica* office where you pay after the call.

For calls within Spain, dial the number of your correspondent, including the area code which is now integrated with the number. For Directory Enquiries dial 1003, International Directory Enquiries 1008 (Europe) and 1009 (rest of the world).

As in most countries, telephone calls made from hotels may be convenient, but they are also very expensive.

Time difference

Spanish standard time is GMT plus one hour. Spanish summer time begins on the last Sunday in March at 2am when the clocks go forward an hour (the same day as British Summer Time), and it ends on the last Sunday in October at 3am

when the clocks go back again.

Tipping

In Spain it is usual to tip between 5-10 per cent of the bill at restaurants, bars, and cafés, even though bills already include a service charge. The tip is related to customer satisfaction so the amount can vary each time, and porters, doormen, taxi drivers and cinema usherettes all expect a financial show of appreciation.

Toilets

There are many names for toilets in Spain, so look out for the following possibilities: *baños* (bathrooms), *aseos*,

A farmhouse in the Serrania de Ronda.

servicios, sanitarios, damas (ladies) or *caballeros* (gentlemen), *señoras* (women) or *señores* (men). Public toilets, which are often quite rare, are usually the old-fashioned squatting type – quite clean but often bereft of paper, so carry your own.

Tourist Information Offices
The Spanish National Tourist Office is an excellent source of information for your holiday, on everything from where to stay in Spain to where and when the lesser known fiestas are held. Offices can be found at the following addresses:

UK
22-23 Manchester Square, London W1M 5AP
☎ **020 7486 8077**.

Canada
102 Bloor Street West, 14th Floor, Toronto, Ontario M5S 1M8 ☎ **416 961 3131**.

Australia
203 Castlereagh Street, Suite 21a, PO Box A685, Sydney, NSW
☎ **02 264 7966**.

USA
665 Fifth Avenue, New York, NY10022 ☎ **212 759 8822**, and Water Tower Place, Suite 915 East, 845 North Michigan Avenue, Chicago, IL 60611
☎ **312 642 1992**.

Tourist information centres (*Junta de Andalucía*) can be found in most large towns and holiday resorts throughout the region, and are known as *turismo*. They are well stocked with maps and information on excursions, transport, entertainment, restaurants and accommodation.

Transport

Andalucia is, for the most part, well served by public transport, with buses and trains often costing the same and journey times being similar. Buses serve the smaller towns and villages well, while local trains – often with stations miles from the towns they serve – tend to travel excruciatingly slowly.

The faster trains, Electrotren, Talgo and Pendular are generally intercity; these are very fast and comfortable, but expensive. The Al-Andalus Express is a particularly luxurious train designed to show off the best of the area to travellers. The high-speed train (AVE) takes just 3 hours from Madrid to Seville.

Several rail passes offer significant reductions on fares, and the Spanish rail company RENFE has 'blue days' – *días azules* – when generous discounts apply. For full details enquire at Spanish Railways

RENFE (☎ 902 24 02 02, www.renfe.es), or Spanish tourist offices in your own country or within the region.

Taxi fares vary in different areas, but taxi drivers should have a list of approved charges for the different runs, and will quote on request before you set off. On top of the basic charge, there is a surcharge for night time, weekends and public holidays.

TV and Radio

The television is usually on in bars and restaurants, so visitors get a good idea of what the Spanish watch. The choice is a mixture of good live sports events, game shows, dubbed foreign language films, and soap operas from Australia, the US, the UK and South America.

English programmes on the BBC World Service can be picked up on short-wave radio, as well as American Forces' stations.

Water

Water is generally safe to drink throughout Spain, although in many places along the Mediterranean coast it may taste salty.

Due to severe drought conditions in many parts of Spain, water restrictions may apply.

INDEX